Maths mastery with greater depth

Year 6

Russell Timmins

Introduction

What is mastery?

'Mastery' is a word that has become a key focus of teaching over the last couple of years.

The essential idea behind mastery is that *all* pupils need a *deep* understanding of the mathematics they are learning to ensure that future mathematical learning is built on solid foundations.

According to the National Centre for Excellence in the Teaching of Mathematics (NCETM), mastery is 'the development of deep structural knowledge and the ability to make connections. Making connections in mathematics deepens knowledge of concepts and procedures, ensures what is learnt is sustained over time, and cuts down the time required to assimilate and master later concepts and techniques.'

What is mastery with greater depth?

Developing mastery with *greater depth* is characterised by pupils' ability to solve problems with greater complexity (where the approach is not immediately obvious) demonstrating an imaginative and creative handling. Pupils working at greater depth can communicate results clearly and explain their understanding to others.

How to use this book

This book includes a set of sophisticated mathematical problems for each National Curriculum requirement. The 100 challenge questions included in the book can be adapted and varied to suit most pupils. Variation is an important factor of mastery. Variation is the art of sequencing similar but increasingly complex problems with the aim of pupils spotting patterns and understanding the underlying structure of the mathematics.

Applying variation to the tasks in the book will mean you can easily extend the problems that you give to pupils. For example, you could vary many of the challenges by simply changing the numbers given for more difficult options. Some activities include suggestions of variation that can be used to further check pupils' understanding.

Detailed answers to all challenges, plus assessment guidance and notes will help you to assess whether pupils are achieving mastery with greater depth. The guidance includes information about what evidence of mastery you might see and suggests questions you could ask which could uncover pupils' thinking. It also includes details of what to check and what that tells you, questioning to prompt or check reasoning and other things to be aware of.

Contents

Acknowledgements

Published by Keen Kite Books
An imprint of HarperCollins*Publishers* Ltd
1 London Bridge Street
London
SE1 9GF

Images and Illustrations are © Shutterstock.com and © HarperCollins*Publishers* Ltd

Text and design © 2016 Keen Kite Books, an imprint of HarperCollins*Publishers* Ltd

10 9 8 7 6 5 4 3 2 1

ISBN 9780008207069

The author asserts their moral right to be identified as the author of this work.

Any educational institution that has purchased one copy of this publication may make duplicate copies for use exclusively within that institution. Permission does not extend to reproduction, storage in a retrieval system or transmission in any form or by any means – electronic, mechanical, photocopying, recording or otherwise – of duplicate copies for lending, renting or selling to any other user or institution without the prior consent, in writing, of the Publisher.

British Library Cataloguing in Publication Data
A catalogue record for this publication is available from the British Library.

Author: Russell Timmins
Commissioning Editor: Michelle I'Anson and Shelley Teasdale
Project Management: Fiona Watson
Cover Design: Anthony Godber
Internal design and illustrations: QBS Learning
Production: Lyndsey Rogers

Number – Number and place value

All in order

Challenge 1: The population of Scotland is roughly 5 295 000.

    a) Write this number in words.

    b) What do the digits 2 and 9 represent in the number?

    c) This number has been rounded to the nearest 1000. Could the real number be higher or lower than this? What could the lowest and highest numbers have been before rounding took place?

    d) Write the answer to 5 295 000 divided by 10 in words.

    e) Write the answer to 5 295 000 multiplied by 10 in words.

Challenge 2: Write the numbers below in order from least value to greatest value.

| 5.1 | 0.501 | 5.105 | −5.15 | −0.55 | 0.005 |

If you multiply each number by 1000 does it alter their order in terms of size?

Challenge 3: Alfie, Barbara, Charlie and Dorothy have cars valued at £14 490, £14 730, £14 820 and £15 040.

Dorothy says: 'My car is not the cheapest of the four cars.'

Alfie says: 'My car's value is the same whether it's rounded to the nearest £100 or £1000.'

Barbara claims that her car is not valued at more than £15 000 but is closer in value to £15 000 than £14 000. She also says that if you round it to the nearest 100, it is the only car value divisible by 37.

Do you have enough information to work out the value of the car belonging to each person? If so, match them.

Challenge 4: Two multimillionaires are comparing their bank account balances. Millionaire A says he has £7.3 million to the nearest £100 000, while millionaire B says she has £7 million to the nearest million. Millionaire A says that he must have the most money in his account.

Do you agree? Explain why he is right or wrong.

National Curriculum objectives, Year 6, Number and place value

- **read, write, order and compare numbers up to 10 000 000 and determine the value of each digit**
- **round any whole number to a required degree of accuracy**
- **use negative numbers in context, and calculate intervals across zero**
- **solve number and practical problems that involve all of the above**

Challenge 1 Answer

a) Five million, two hundred and ninety-five thousand

b) 2 represents two hundred thousand and 9 represents ninety thousand

c) The real numbers could be higher or lower. The lowest possible number is 5 294 500 and the greatest possible number is 5 295 499.

d) Five hundred and twenty-nine thousand, five hundred

e) Fifty-two million, nine hundred and fifty thousand

Assessment

Check that pupils know that the actual size of the digit in any number is determined by its position and not the value of the digit alone. In (b) they should know that 2 < 9 but 200 000 > 90 000.

Question them about why a number rounded to the nearest 1000 is 5 295 000 and what the bounds of that number are (500 smaller or 500 greater); in this case 5 294 500 and 5 295 499.999. How does this reasoning affect numbers to the nearest 10 or 100?

Ask pupils to tell you about the digits in a number after division or multiplication by a power of 10 to check that they understand that the digits do not change nor do they change order.

How are they performing routine calculations in this challenge? Look out for pupils using formal written methods when mental methods are more efficient. In problems (d) and (e), encourage pupils to write their answers in digits separated in clusters of three from the right to support writing the numbers in words and identifying the value of each digit.

Challenge 2 Answer

−5.15, −0.55, 0.005, 0.501, 5.1, 5.105

Pupils should have explained that multiplying each number does not alter the order they appear in.

Assessment

Check that pupils are able to organise the numbers into two separate groups (positive and negative) for ordering purposes.

Do they use an empty number line separated by the zero place holder to arrange the numbers? Are they able to label each end of the number line with the lowest and highest values?

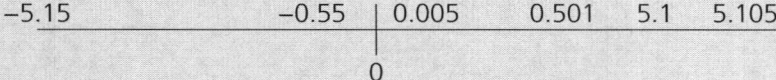

Do they organise the negative and positive numbers in order on either side of zero?

Make sure that pupils understand that the greater (absolute value of) a negative or positive number, the further away from zero it is placed. Make sure they realise that multiplying or dividing these numbers will not affect their order.

Challenge 3 Answer

Yes, there is enough information.

Alfie: £15 040, Barbara: £14 820, Charlie: £14 490, Dorothy: £14 730

Assessment

This challenge relies heavily on pupils' ability to round and compare numbers with some long division linked to the problem-solving process. There is also a logical element that impacts on decision making in the problem-solving elements.

Check how pupils initially access the problem. Do they start by writing out the values of the cars and rounding them to the nearest £100 and £1000 to work out which value relates to Alfie's car (£15 040)?

Do they understand that to work out the value of Barbara's car, they need to refer to the remaining values rounded to the nearest 100 (£14 500, £14 700 and £14 800)? As they are all multiples of 100, they can divide 145, 147 and 148 by 37 to identify the correct value of Barbara's car. Are they using formal long division methods or finding factors of each of the three numbers to see if 37 is one?

Can they explain that there is enough information from Dorothy's statement of her car not being the lowest in value to work out how much her car and Charlie's car are worth? Hence there is enough information to work out who owns each car.

Challenge 4 Answer

Millionaire A could have any amount between and including £7 250 000 and £7 349 999.99.

Millionaire B could have any amount between and including £6 500 000 and £7 499 999.99.

Millionaire A is wrong to think that he must have more money in his account than millionaire B.

Assessment

Check that pupils are able to apply what they know about rounding to round to the nearest 1 000 000.

Can they argue that when a number is rounded to the nearest 100 000 it could be 50 000 less or just under 50 000 more?

Can pupils argue that if a number was rounded to the nearest million it could be 500 000 less or just under 500 000 more?

Number – Number and place value

Negative numbers and rounding

Challenge 5: Two towns have the following populations: 67 105 and 38 295.

    a) Calculate their combined populations:

        i) rounding both amounts to the nearest 1000

        ii) rounding both amounts to the nearest 100

        iii) rounding both amounts to the nearest 10

        iv) rounding both amounts to the nearest 10 000.

    b) If you round numbers to a greater degree of accuracy you will get closer to the real value. Do you agree or disagree with this statement? Explain your reasoning.

Challenge 6: The depth of one mineshaft was measured as –250m. The second had a depth of –75m. A third mineshaft was three times as deep as the second.

    a) Which mineshaft is the deepest?

    b) There is an engine tower at the top of the first mineshaft. It is $\frac{1}{5}$ as tall as the shaft is deep. What is the distance from the top of the tower to the bottom of the shaft?

Challenge 7: The temperature in Paris at 11am on 1 January was 4.7°C. The temperature at 11pm on the same day was –15.3°C.

    a) What was the temperature range between the two times on that day?

    b) If both temperatures were 11.8°C higher one month later, what would they be?

Challenge 8: A computer factory employs 400 workers to the nearest 100 and they all eat lunch every day at the on-site cafeteria. They each spend £6 to the nearest 50p on lunch.

    a) Estimate the total daily lunchtime takings in the cafeteria.

    b) Would you argue that your calculation is more than, less than or exactly the amount taken?

National Curriculum objectives, Year 6, Number and place value

- *read, write, order and compare numbers up to 10 000 000 and determine the value of each digit*
- *round any whole number to a required degree of accuracy*
- *use negative numbers in context, and calculate intervals across zero*
- *solve number and practical problems that involve all of the above*

Challenge 5 Answer

a)

i) 67 000 + 38 000 = 105 000

ii) 67 100 + 38 300 = 105 400

iii) 67 110 + 38 300 = 105 410

iv) 70 000 + 40 000 = 110 000

b) In general, the smaller the rounding, the nearer to the true value, but sometimes two different roundings can give the same result. (An example should be given to back this up.)

Assessment

Make sure pupils understand how rounding works from a number line model. For example:

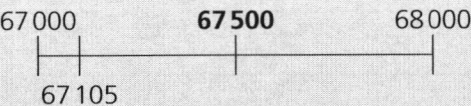

Are they using an understood rule about whether a number is rounded up or down? For example, do they understand that a number rounded to the nearest 1000 on a number line (above) would have two possible results (67 000 or 68 000) and that the half way point (67 500) should be labelled, followed by a placing of the original number in the appropriate 'half'?

Check this understanding by asking them which number to the nearest hundred 37 would round to and why.

Once you have established that pupils have a good understanding of rounding, make sure they are correctly rounding and systematically checking answers to the addition questions through use of an inverse operation.

Question pupils to make sure they can justify the answer that the smaller the rounding bounds, the closer to the original number the result will be, even if rounding to the nearest 10 or 100 gives identical results (e.g. 97 rounded to the nearest 10 and the nearest 100).

Challenge 6 Answer

a) The first mineshaft is deepest at −250m. (The third mineshaft is only 225m deep or −225m.)

b) 300m

Assessment

Make sure that the negative value of the depth of the shafts is understood as an absolute value. The understanding of negative numbers to this point has been that they are smaller than their positive counterparts. This real-world example shows that negative numbers can also be used to understand a particular mathematical event, in this case a depth from ground zero as opposed to a height.

Check that without actually using the term 'absolute value', pupils are able to add the whole number measurements.

Make sure that pupils understand that although some measurements are given negative values, no subtraction is needed when calculating total depths.

Are pupils linking the fraction $\frac{1}{5}$ to a division by 5 in order to calculate the measurement relating to the tower from the information given about the mineshaft depth?

Are they using formal written or mental methods for their calculations and can they justify their choices?

Challenge 7 Answer

a) 20°C

b) 4.7 + 11.8 = 16.5°C, −15.3 + 11.8 = −3.5°C

Assessment

Can pupils explain what is meant by 'temperature range'?

Building on the previous challenge, are they using absolute number values to calculate results? For example, in (a) do they know that the range is found by calculating 4.7 + 15.3, which comes from 4.7 −(−15.3)?

Ask them to explain how they are calculating a rise in temperature of 11.8°C from a starting temperature of −15.3°C. Are they using number lines or are they using a more fluent approach based on the understanding that −15.3 + 11.8 is equal to 11.8 − 15.3 or better −(15.3 − 11.8)?

Challenge 8 Answer

a) £2400

b) It could be more than, less than or exactly the amount taken.

Assessment

Do pupils see that to answer part (a) it is necessary only to multiply £6 by 400 to get an acceptable estimate of daily takings?

Check how they are getting £2400 as the result. Is it through formal or mental calculation? Ask them why they chose their particular method.

Question (b) relies on mathematical reasoning. Ask pupils to justify whether the sum £2400 could be the actual day's takings and how likely the possibility would be. Expect them to explain that it is highly unlikely as both figures used to calculate this sum are rounded. Ask them to justify why it could be much higher or lower than this figure. Pupils should realise that the £6 could be as low as £5.75 or as high as £6.24. Not only this, but the number of workers could be 350 or 449. Having reasoned what the real figures could be, ask pupils to use formal multiplication methods or mental calculations to show low and high figures, based on how the rounding affects the numbers. A good example of fluency would be to multiply £5.75 by 350 to find the lowest figure (£2012.50) and then to multiply £6.24 by 449 to get the highest figure (£2801.76).

Number – Addition and subtraction

Getting into columns

Challenge 1: Nacho says that before he adds two numbers such as 58 and 72, he first rounds them to 60 and 70 so he knows the result will be approximately 130. Find a way of using this idea to help you solve the following problems. Use column methods of addition and subtraction when not using a mental method.

a) 2194 + 3128

b) 219.4 + 312.8

c) 4221 – 2147

d) 2186.2 – 534.4

Challenge 2: Solve the following problems using an efficient method. Explain how an estimation for each solution could be helpful. For question (d), convince your teacher that you know you have the correct result by using the result and applying what you know about inverse operations.

a) 15.7 + 9.4

b) 26.8 + 113.6

c) 106.4 – 57.2

d) 601.3 – 256.8

Challenge 3: Identify the missing digit in each problem. Use a systematic approach.

a) 4 ☐ 2 + 221 = 703

b) 19 ☐ 7 – 408 = 1559

c) 18.5 – ☐ .68 = 10.82

d) 4 ☐ 8.3 + 19.8 = 478.1

Challenge 4: A school had to order two minibuses to take two teachers and a number of children on a trip. The minibuses each hold 15 passengers. Adult tickets cost £8.50 and pupil tickets cost £5.20. Only one teacher is allowed on each minibus.

a) If at least one of the minibuses was full, and neither teacher was a lone passenger, what is the smallest total number of adults and children that went on the trip? Explain your reasoning.

b) If the total value of tickets sold was £126.20, how many pupils went on the trip? Use an approximation method before solving this.

- *solve addition and subtraction multi-step problems in contexts, deciding which operations and methods to use and why*
- *use estimation to check answers to calculations and determine, in the context of a problem, an appropriate degree of accuracy*

Challenge 1 Answer

a) $2194 + 3128 \approx 2190 + 3130 = 5320; 2194 + 3128 = 5322$

b) $219.4 + 312.8 \approx 219 + 313 = 532; 219.4 + 312.8 = 532.2$

c) $4221 - 2147 \approx 4220 - 2150 = 2070; 4221 - 2147 = 2074$

d) $2186.2 - 534.4 \approx 2190 - 530 = 1660; 2186.2 - 534.4 = 1651.8$

Assessment

Check that pupils are rounding the numbers in (a) and (c) to the nearest 10. Are they rounding the numbers in (b) to the nearest whole number and in (d) to the nearest 10? Are some pupils arguing that because of the decimal point, a closer rounding is needed? How do they justify this if so? Ask them if rounding to the nearest 10 still achieves the goal of finding a close result.

Are they able to reason that, as all the numbers involved in (b) are 10 times smaller than those in (a), the result will also be 10 times smaller? Some pupils may write this explanation in place of a column method of addition.

Check that pupils are using mental methods for the rounded calculations and column methods for the actual calculations of the given numbers.

Challenge 2 Answer

a) $15.7 + 9.4 = 25.1$

b) $26.8 + 113.6 = 140.4$

c) $106.4 - 57.2 = 49.2$

d) $601.3 - 256.8 = 344.5$

Assessment

If pupils have completed these using the column method, ask them to work through them again using a mental calculation strategy. Strategies to look out for include rounding and adjusting, for example, $15.7 + 10 = 25.7$, $25.7 - 0.6 = 25.1$ and sequencing, for example, $106.4 - 50 - 7 - 0.2$. Pupils need to decide which are the most efficient ways to calculate and not always simply carry out column methods. Ensure that you provide opportunities to practise mental calculation strategies.

Check that pupils have estimated the answers by rounding the numbers appropriately. Do they understand that an approximated answer gives a good guide to the exact result? If they haven't used estimation, this is something that you will need to work on in class. Many pupils just want to give an answer straight away. Estimating is a life skill and pupils need to get into the habit of doing it.

Are they able to achieve an accurate result by column subtraction for (d) and check it independently by using the inverse operation?

Challenge 3 Answer

a) 8   **b)** 6   **c)** 7   **d)** 5

Assessment

Question pupils about their reasoning when completing question (a). Did they reason that the problem could be simplified to 70 − 22 in order to find the unknown digit (8)?

In question (b), look for pupils reasoning that the solution is found from 1559 + 408.

In general, for all questions, look for pupils' fluency using inverse operations in order to find the complete number where a digit is unknown. For example, in (c) and (d):

$$
\begin{array}{r}
18.5 \\
-\ 10.82 \\
\hline
7.68
\end{array}
\qquad
\begin{array}{r}
478.1 \\
-\ 19.8 \\
\hline
458.3
\end{array}
$$

Challenge 4 Answer

a) 2 teachers and 15 pupils

b) 2 teachers and 21 pupils went on the trip.

Assessment

In problem (a), check that pupils have understood that there are two, and only two, teachers and that there must be more than 14 pupils going on the trip otherwise the second teacher would be a lone passenger. Did they reason that there must be one full minibus (14 pupils and one teacher) and therefore the smallest number on the trip would be one extra pupil plus a teacher on the second minibus, so two teachers and 15 pupils in total?

For problem (b), have they calculated the cost of the people on one minibus (1 adult @ £8.50 + 14 pupils @ £5.20 = £81.30) then subtracted this from the total figure of £126.20 (£44.90)? Check that they then subtracted the cost of a teacher from £44.90 (= £36.40) and divided £36.40 by £5.20 to find that seven pupils and one teacher were on the second coach, so two teachers and 21 pupils altogether. Check that pupils are reasoning that 36.40 ÷ 5.20 is the same as 364 ÷ 52 – this shows a high level of mastery and understanding of the rules of division. Or did they subtract £17 from £126.20 and then divide to find how many pupil tickets?

Note the methods pupils used to work this out. Some will reason that problem (b) can be solved algebraically: A = £8.50 and P = £5.20 with the unknown variable being the number of pupils. They will reason that as there is only one variable, a solution can be found. They will convert the information using A for adult and P for pupil into $2A + nP = 2(£8.50) + n(£5.20) = £126.20$.

Number — Addition and subtraction

All in order

Challenge 5: Anja visited the petrol station twice in two weeks. She spent £50.42 in week 1 and £8.84 less in week 2.

    a) Use a mental method and explain how you would calculate how much Anja spent on petrol in the two-week period.

    b) Check your mental calculation with a column method of subtraction *only* (so there will also be a need for some mental calculation).

    c) Explain which method is the most efficient in solving this problem.

Challenge 6: Finding the difference between two numbers means finding the 'distance' between the two numbers on a number line. If we add or subtract the same number to or from the two numbers in a given subtraction, the distance stays the same. Explain how you would use this knowledge to mentally solve the following.

    a) 152 – 87

    b) 2311 – 178

    c) 5319 – 3561

Challenge 7:

I am thinking of two numbers. When I add them their total is 7. The difference between my two numbers is exactly 1.4. What are the two numbers I am thinking of?

Challenge 8:

A pencil and an eraser cost 83p. The pencil costs 25p less than the eraser. How much change from a £5 note would I get if I bought three pencils and two erasers?

- *solve addition and subtraction multi-step problems in contexts, deciding which operations and methods to use and why*
- *use estimation to check answers to calculations and determine, in the context of a problem, an appropriate degree of accuracy*
- *perform mental calculations, including with mixed operations and large numbers*

Challenge 5 Answer

The cost over two weeks was £92.

Assessment

a) An effective mental calculation method, but not the only one, would be to double £50.42 (£100.84) and then subtract £8.84 (£92).

b) Notice how the two-step problem was approached. Look for a mixture of mental and written calculation, in particular the sum of £50.42 being doubled mentally to £100.84, followed by a column method of subtraction only, which eliminates the need for column addition. Check that pupils' understanding and use of formal subtraction procedures is in order.

c) Check that pupils have understood that the mental method is the quickest and most efficient. Ask them their thoughts on whether a calculation should be carried out in a formal written way first before looking at mental possibilities.

Note: The numbers chosen for this problem enabled such reasoning, but pupils could be challenged to state whether the same approach would be as successful if the figure £50.42 was changed to £47.63. Develop this by asking what adjustments might have to be made.

Challenge 6 Answer

a) e.g. add 3 to both numbers, 155 – 90 = 65

b) e.g. add 22 to both numbers, 2333 – 200 = 2133

c) e.g. add 39 to both numbers, 5358 – 3600 = 1758

Assessment

Check that pupils' explanations are based on turning the number to be subtracted into a tens number by making an equal adjustment to the number from which it is to be subtracted. So in (a), 3 can be added to both numbers so the calculation becomes 155 – 90, while (b) could become 2313 – 180.

Pupils demonstrating higher mastery in (b) will have mentally added 22 to both numbers so that the calculation becomes 2333 – 200, making for an easier mental calculation than 2313 – 180.

Check that although the question asks for mental calculations, pupils understand that jottings are allowed.

In question (c), check for higher levels of mastery with the attempted use of subtraction as opposed to addition in their adjustments. 5318 – 3560 gives a number ending in zero to be subtracted, but it is not that straightforward to calculate mentally. A more efficient method would be to add 39 (with jottings), giving 5358 – 3600. Adding 400 would make the calculation easier: 5758 – 400.

Challenge 7 Answer

2.8 and 4.2

Assessment

Pupils may be able to see that (algebraically) this problem can be represented as 'two identical numbers plus 1.4 is equal to 7'. The bar method will show a tangible model of this.

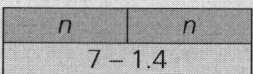

Pupils may have drawn this model to show that they subtract 1.4 from 7 and halve the answer to find the value of n.

If pupils are able to see the problem in algebraic terms as above, then they should be able to subtract 1.4 from 7 leaving 5.6 and know that this is the sum of the two identical numbers.

Check that they then find the numbers 2.8 and (2.8 + 1.4 = 4.2).

The bar model is an effective problem-solving tool. It enables pupils to see the structure of the mathematics they are working on. If you haven't embedded its use in your school, it would be a good idea to ensure you do.

Discuss other approaches pupils may have taken to solving this problem. Ask them to create a similar problem based on this algebraic reasoning to see if you (the teacher) can solve it.

Challenge 8 Answer

£3.05

Assessment

Check that pupils have reasoned that in algebraic terms 83p is also the sum of 2 pencils plus 25p and so by subtracting 25p from 83p (58p) followed by a division by 2 (pencils) they can find the value of 1 pencil being 29p. Given this, they are able to calculate the value of the eraser as 54p.

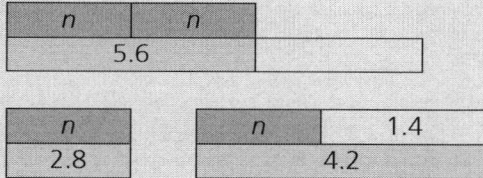

Check that they double check this result by adding 54p to 29p.

Ask pupils if they thought mental calculations, formal written calculations or a mixture was the best way to solve the problem of change from a £5 note.

High levels of mastery will be observed from pupils solving by mental methods alone.

$$3(29p) = 3(30p) - 3p = £0.87$$

$$2(54p) = £1.08$$

$$£0.87 + £1.08 = £1.95$$

$$£5.00 - £1.95 = £3.05$$

Number – Multiplication and division

Scaling up and down

Challenge 1: Here is a multiplication fact: 23 × 312 = 7176.

Use this fact to mentally solve the following problems.

a) 2.3 × 312

b) 230 × 31.2

c) 0.23 × 3.12

d) 717.6 ÷ 2.3

e) 3588 ÷ 31.2

Challenge 2: Carlotta says that the result of 5 × 4 – 12 ÷ 6 + 2 is the same as 5 × 4.

a) Do you agree? Explain why you think she is wrong or right.

b) She also believes that (15 ÷ 3) + (2 × 7) – (5 – 2) = 16 is true even without the brackets. Explain why you think she is right or wrong.

Challenge 3: Find numbers that go into the empty boxes to make each statement true. Problems (a) and (b) must contain 2 two-digit whole numbers and (c) must contain at least 1 two-digit whole number in the second box.

a) ☐ × ☐ = 351

b) ☐ × ☐ = 693

c) ☐ ÷ ☐ = 27

d) Jan says that there is only one answer for each of the first two problems, but 10 answers for problem (c). Explain why you agree or disagree with Jan.

Challenge 4: In a year that has 365 days, 13 January falls on a Wednesday.

a) What day of the week will 4 June fall on?

b) If the following year also has 365 days, what day of the week will 20 January fall on?

Challenge 1 Answer

a) 717.6   **b)** 7176   **c)** 0.7176   **d)** 312   **e)** 115

Assessment

Pupils should reason that the first three problems use the same digits in the same order and use knowledge of powers of 10 to solve the problems. Some pupils may use estimation to achieve the correct answer, e.g. d) $700 \div 2 \approx 350$ so answer 312.

a) Check that pupils understand that the answer to this problem (717.6) is 10 times smaller than the answer to the sample multiplication fact given ($23 \times 312 = 7176$).

b) Good levels of mastery are demonstrated if pupils realise that the first number is 10 times larger than the original first number and the second 10 times smaller than the original second number, which cancels out any changes to the original result.

c) Check that pupils use the previous reasoning to realise that the result must be 100×100 (10000) times smaller than 7176 (0.7176).

d) Look for reasoning that the result must contain 3, 1 and 2 in this order. Pupils should realise that 717.6 is 10 times smaller and 2.3 is also 10 times smaller and therefore a division of the larger number by the smaller gives the same result as the original.

e) Check that they reasoned that 3588 is either a factor or multiple of either 7176 or 23. In this case, it is half of 7176 and, as such, the result will be half the result of $7176 \div 31.2$ (this is equal to $230 \div 2 = 115$).

Pupils demonstrating mathematical fluency will use knowledge and understanding of **if $ab = c$ then $a = \frac{c}{b}$ and $b = \frac{c}{a}$** to rearrange the equations given in order to apply what is known from the original statement ($23 \times 312 = 7176$). They will use increasing confidence in a more algebraic approach to problem solving of this kind.

Challenge 2 Answer

a) Carlotta is correct.   **b)** Carlotta is incorrect, without brackets the result is 12.

Assessment

Ability to complete (a) depends on mathematical reasoning and an understanding of order of operations (multiplication and division are operations that take priority over addition and subtraction). Pupils should explain that '$-12 \div 6 + 2$' is actually $-2 + 2 = 0$.

In (b) they will again need to reason their answer through their understanding of order of operations and show that results of a multi-operation problem will vary if order of operations is not adhered to. Check that they find a solution to the problem as it is set out ($5 + 14 - 3 = 16$) followed by a solution without brackets ($15 \div 3 + 2 \times 7 - 5 - 2$). Pupils should explain that while the first two sets of brackets are unnecessary, removing the last pair changes the final step of the calculation from $- 3$ to $- 7$.

Ask them if it is possible to have a string of operations including brackets that gives the same result as with brackets removed. For example, $(2 \times 3) + 7 - (24 \div 8) = 6 + 7 - 3 = 10 = 2 \times 3 + 7 - 24 \div 8$. Try to get them to see what it was in the question's example that differs from a result like in this previous example where brackets are irrelevant.

Challenge 3 Answer

a) 13×27 **b)** 21×33 or 11×63

c) $p \div q = 27$ implying $27q = p$. If $q = 10$, for example, then $p = 270$. Many other answers are possible.

d) Jan is correct to say that there is only one solution for (a), but there are two for (b). She is also wrong about (c) as there are many possibilities.

Assessment

Pupils should show an understanding of how all whole numbers contain two or more factors and use this to search out factors based on specified characteristics. For example, pupils are told that (a) and (b) must each contain 2 two-digit numbers. Look for them using the reasoning that they need to find all the factors of 351 and 693 and then find one pair of two-digit factors for each one.

A higher level of mastery when used in a fluent problem-solving way would be the beginnings of the use of prime factors, from which multiple factors can be constructed.

3	351
3	117
3	39
13	13

3	693
3	231
7	77
11	11

$$13 \times (3 \times 3 \times 3) = 13 \times 27$$

$$11 \times (7 \times 3 \times 3) = 11 \times 63$$
$$(11 \times 3) \times (7 \times 3) = 33 \times 21$$

In (c) they should reason that they can have any two-digit number they want in the second box as, through inverse operations, this number multiplied by 27 dictates the result of the first unknown number. Take, for instance, the second box having the value 11, then the first box is the result of 27×11 (297).

In (d) pupils will rely heavily on mathematical reasoning and knowledge of factors to justify their answer. They will argue that there is only one result for (a) as there is only one combination of the prime factors of 351 that creates 2 two-digit numbers (13, 27). The same reasoning will help them to prove that the conjecture is false for (b). In (c), if they can prove this without calculations it will show a high level of mastery. They only have to find one number which is two-digits, which effectively allows the second box to be any number from and including 10 to 99.

Challenge 4 Answer

a) 4 June will be a Friday. **b)** 20 January next year will be a Thursday.

Assessment

Pupils could laboriously count the dates until they get to 4 June in (a), but this does not show a fluency of approach. They should be able to mentally calculate that there are 18 days until the end of January and then add this to the number of days until 4 June ($18 + 28 + 31 + 30 + 31 + 4 = 142$). Dividing this number by 7 and expressing the answer as a mixed number gives $20\frac{2}{7}$. They will reason that the fractional part of the answer represents the number of days out of a seven-day week and reason that the week starts on Wednesday as given in the question and therefore the extra $\frac{2}{7}$ of a week makes 4 June a Friday.

In part (b), they will use the fact that in any consecutive non-leap year the date is always one weekday later. This makes 13 January the following year a Thursday and therefore 20 January will also be a Thursday.

Number – Multiplication and division

Factors and problems

Challenge 5: **a)** How many ways can you find to solve this problem using whole numbers only? Are you sure you have found them all?

$\boxed{} \times \boxed{} = 420$

b) Find at least six different ways to solve this problem.

$\boxed{} \times \boxed{} \times \boxed{} = 420$

Challenge 6: The diagram shows how the grid method of multiplication links very closely to column multiplication.

	2000	300	10	2	
20	40000	6000	200	40	46240
1	2000	300	10	2	+ 2312
					48552

```
  2312      (2312 × 2 × 10)
×   21
46240
+ 2312
48552      (2312 × 1)
```

a) Solve 1263 × 32 using the grid method, then place the information from your grid into a formal column method.

b) Solve 2524 × 22 using the formal column method only.

Challenge 7: A box of eggs at a cash and carry costs £30.72. Each box contains 8 trays and each tray holds 48 eggs.

How much does one egg cost? Show how you solved this problem without a calculator.

Challenge 8: Carmen bought 17 raffle tickets at the school fete and paid for them with a £10 note. Her change was three different silver coins.

How much did each raffle ticket cost?

National Curriculum objectives, Year 6, Multiplication and division

- *divide numbers up to 4 digits by a two-digit whole number using the formal written method of long division, and interpret remainders as whole number remainders, fractions, or by rounding, as appropriate for the context*
- *multiply multi-digit numbers up to 4 digits by a two-digit whole number using the formal written method of long multiplication*
- *identify common factors, common multiples and prime numbers*

Challenge 5 Answer

a) 12 ways. There are 12 factor pairs of 420 (1 × 420, 2 × 210, 3 × 140, 4 × 105, 5 × 84, 6 × 70, 7 × 60, 10 × 42, 12 × 35, 14 × 30, 15 × 28, 20 × 21).

b) 420 can be represented as 2 × 2 × 3 × 5 × 7 and therefore any mixture of three multiples of this will work, for example 4 × 3 × 35 and 6 × 7 × 10.

Assessment

Pupils should reason that by finding the real factors of 420 then all possible number pairs can be found. In (a) they should be expected to use a systematic approach to find all of them by pairing up the factors from the extremities in turn: (1, 420), (2, 210), (3, 140) and so on. They should be able to state with confidence that there are 12 pairs of factors.

A systematic approach to (b) will be seen when it is known that one of a given pair of factors might be able to be factorised further, leaving a total of three factors altogether. Check that pupils have taken two factor pairs found in (a) and then broken one of them into two further factor pairs. For example:

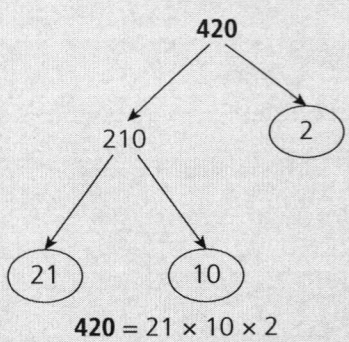

$420 = 21 \times 10 \times 2$

Challenge 6 Answer

a)

	1000	200	60	3	
30	30000	6000	1800	90	37890
2	2000	400	120	6	+ 2526

40416
1 1 1

```
    1
  1263      (1263 × 3 × 10)
 ×  32
 37890
+ 2526      (1263 × 2)
 40416
  1 1 1
```

b)

```
    1
  2524      (2524 × 2 × 10)
 ×  22
 50480
+ 5048      (2524 × 2)
 55528
    1
```

Assessment

Check that pupils can organise the numbers into a grid and complete the smaller multiplications suggested by it. After adding each row, they should be able to convert this information to a column representation without need for calculation at that point as it is a simple transfer of information.

Check that they annotate their work to show, for example, how in the column method 1263 × 30 is the same as 1263 × 3 × 10. Check that they are influenced by this annotation to try to express 2524 × 22 as 2524 × 2 × 10 for the first row result of 5048 × 10 = 50 480, followed by 2524 × 2 = 5048. The mixing of mental and formal written methods is an example of fluent application in problem solving.

Challenge 7 Answer

One egg costs 8p.

Assessment

This challenge provides an opportunity to check that pupils are able to solve a problem with the use of formal division and possibly formal column multiplication, although mental methods of multiplication are also possible.

Check that pupils are completing the division in steps: £30.72 = 3072 ÷ 48 = 64, so 64p per tray; 64 ÷ 8 = 8, so 8p per egg. Pupils could use a formal method or repeated division, using their knowledge of tables.

$$
\begin{array}{r}
6\,4 \\
48\,\overline{)3\,0\,7\,2} \\
-2\,8\,8 \\
\hline
1\,9\,2 \\
1\,9\,2 \\
\hline
0
\end{array}
\qquad 6\,4 \div 8 = \mathbf{8}
$$

Make sure that after arriving at the cost of an egg (8p) they check this by multiplying it by 384 (48 × 8), which should get them back to the cost of a box of eggs (£30.72).

mental multiplication **48 × 8** = (40 × 8) + (8 × 8) = 320 + 64 = **384**

384 × 8 = (300 × 8) + (80 × 8) + (4 × 8) = 2400 + 640 + 32 = **3072**

Challenge 8 Answer

The cost of one ticket is 55p.

Assessment

Check that pupils systematically find all possible combinations of three different British silver coins and record each sum (50p + 20p + 10p = 80p; 50p + 20p + 5p = 75p; 50p + 10p + 5p = 65p; 20p + 10p + 5p = 35p).

They should then subtract each of these in turn from £10 (or 1000p), which would show the possible cost of 17 tickets to be 965p, 935p, 925p or 920p.

Check the procedures pupils now use to calculate the cost of one raffle ticket. Do they use long division methods or do they link the problem to factors and work out which of the possible total amounts has a factor of 17?

$$
\begin{array}{r}
5\,6 \\
17\,\overline{)9\,6\,5} \\
-8\,5 \\
\hline
1\,1\,5 \\
1\,0\,2 \\
\hline
1\,3
\end{array}
$$

965 ÷ 17 = 56 r 13

17 is not a factor of **965** so the change from a **£10** note cannot be equivalent to three silver coins

(**Long division**)

1000 − 935 = 65

5	935
11	187
17	17
	1

17 is a factor of **935** so the change from a **£10** note has to be **65p** and the cost of one ticket is 55p

(**Prime factor decomposition**)

Number – Addition/subtraction and multiplication/division

More than one operation

Challenge 1: Five friends went to a local theme park. Three bought day entry tickets which cost £32.75 each. The other two bought all-in-one package tickets which cost £49.25 each.

    a) How much did it cost for the five friends to get into the theme park?

    b) Prices for the day entry tickets went up this week. If the friends had gone last week their total entry cost would have been £192.85. How much were the day entry tickets last week?

Challenge 2: Anthony, Beatrice and Carly each saved £28, £36 and £32 respectively each month for 12 months to buy a television that cost the exact amount they saved. On the day they went to buy the television, it had been reduced by £108.

    a) How much did they pay for the television?

    b) Anthony says they should divide the £108 by 3 so they all get £36. Carly says this wouldn't be fair. How do you think the saving should be divided?

Challenge 3: Chelsea, Manchester United and Newcastle United recorded the following respective crowd attendances: 68 912, 71 437 and 49 119. On the same day, Leicester City recorded 564 fewer spectators than the mean of the first three teams.

    a) How many spectators went to watch Leicester City?

    b) What was the mean number of spectators of the four teams?

Challenge 4: Ned is well known in his village for making untrue statements.

> It is not possible that six consecutive months in any single year can be exactly the length of half a year. In a leap year, however, it is possible.

Do you agree with Ned's statements?

- *solve problems involving addition, subtraction, multiplication and division*
- *use estimation to check answers to calculations and determine, in the context of the problem, an appropriate degree of accuracy*

Challenge 1 Answer

a)   £196.75   **b)**   £31.45

Assessment

Pupils should use a multiplication method of their choice to find the cost of the two sets of tickets, then add the results to solve part (a). 3 × £32.75 = £98.25 and 2 × £49.25 = £98.50, so the total for five tickets is £196.75. Check for independent fluent application of mental multiplication at this stage, especially for the cost of the two tickets.

In part (b), check that pupils are first subtracting last week's cost from this week's (£196.75 – £192.85 = £3.90). They should be able to divide this result by 3 to work out how much the cost of a single ticket has increased by (£1.30) and subtract this from £32.75 to find the cost of the day tickets last week (£31.45).

Fluency of approach will see the use of mental and/or formal multiplication of decimal numbers by a whole number and formal addition and subtraction methods. Checking answers by using inverse operations would be a further sign of fluency of approach.

$$
\begin{array}{cc}
 & \text{Increase of one ticket} \\
\begin{array}{r} 19\overset{5}{6}.\overset{1}{7}5 \\ -192.85 \\ \hline 3.90 \end{array} & \qquad \begin{array}{r} 32.75 \\ -1.30 \\ \hline 31.45 \end{array} \\
\end{array}
$$

Total cost of increase → 3.90   of three one-day tickets

1.30
3) 3.90

31.45 ← Price of day ticket last week

___

Challenge 2 Answer

a)   The television cost £1044.

b)   Carly is correct, it is not fair to share the saving of £108 in the way Anthony suggests. The fairest way would be to share it in the same ratio that they saved for 12 months, which would mean Anthony gets £31.50, Beatrice £40.50 and Carly £36.

Assessment

In part (a), pupils should add the three amounts saved each month, then multiply the result by 12 to get a figure saved of £1152. Following this, they should subtract the discount of £108 to find how much they paid for the television (£1044).

In part (b), check that pupils understand that Anthony's suggested distribution of the £108 discount is not fair as simply dividing by three does not reflect the ratio of individual savings each month.

Make sure that they understand that this becomes a ratio problem and that the £108 must be divided in the ratio 28:36:32.

Have pupils reduced the ratio to its simplest form (7:9:8), divided £108 by the total of the ratio values (£108 ÷ 24 = 4.5) and finally multiplied each number of parts by 4.5 to arrive at how the discount should be shared (£31.50:£40.50:£36)?

Ensure they have checked their answer by summing these amounts to £108.

Challenge 3 Answer

a) 62 592 went to see Leicester City.

b) The mean number of spectators of the four teams was 63 015.

Assessment

Pupils should know that the mean is the sum of considered data divided by the number of data entries. In this problem, they should have calculated (68 912 + 71 437 + 49 119) ÷ 3 = 63 156. They should then subtract 564 from this mean figure to find the gate at Leicester City (62 592). Pupils should be aware that formal addition, division and subtraction methods will help to solve the problem through successive small steps.

Check that they have added the gate figure at Leicester to the sum of the other three teams (252 060) followed by a division by four to arrive at the mean figure for the four teams (63 015).

Pupils will probably lay out the information given about the first three teams as a column addition followed by a formal division by 3. They will then use column subtraction to calculate the gate at Leicester City. Talk to them about the methods they have used and ask them to explain why they have chosen them.

$$
\begin{array}{r}
68\,912 \\
71\,437 \\
+\,49\,119 \\
\hline
189\,468 \\
\scriptstyle 1\ 1\ \ \ 1
\end{array}
\qquad
\begin{array}{r}
\mathbf{63156} \\
\hline
3\,|\,189\,4^{1}6^{1}8
\end{array}
\qquad
\begin{array}{r}
\scriptstyle 2\ 10\ 0\ 1 \\
6\,3\,\cancel{1}\,5\,6 \\
-\ 564 \\
\hline
\mathbf{62592}
\end{array}
$$

Challenge 4 Answer

Ned is correct in his first statement: there are 365 days in a whole year; as this is not an even number, it cannot be divided into two sets of equal days.

Ned is also correct about a leap year, which has 366 days. Half of this is 183 days, which is exactly the amount of days from 1 April to 30 September or from 1 June to 30 November.

Assessment

Strong mathematical reasoning in relation to the first statement will be demonstrated by the absence of any calculations. Pupils should argue that a year consists of an odd number of days (365) and therefore there cannot be an exact whole number of days that is equal to a half year because an odd number can never be divided by 2 without a remainder. So a calculation is not needed.

Ned's second statement about the leap year requires more mathematics.

Check that pupils know that the first objective is to calculate the number of days in half a leap year (366 ÷ 2 = 183).

Check their reasoning by asking them how many 31-day months can be in this sum. Pupils should not give a response of four or five (four would mean that the sum is an even number [4 odds + 2 evens = even] and therefore not 183 and it cannot be five as there are not five 31-day months in any six-month period). From this, they need only consider three 31-day months as there are not five 30-day months in any six-month period.

They should now multiply 31 by 3 (93) and subtract this from 183 (90) leaving three 30-day months.

They now need to search for any six-month period containing three months of 30 days and three months of 31 days: April to September or June to November.

Number – Fractions (including decimals and percentages)

Common factors and multiples

Challenge 1: A, B and C are equal lengths made up from different sets of smaller rods joined end-to-end. Each of the smaller rods within a set is identical. No two sets of rods are the same. The ends of each of the rods in A and B line up with the ends of one of the rods in C.

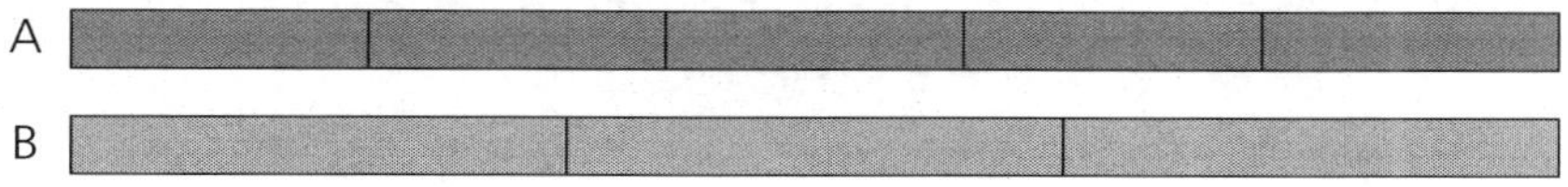

a) Draw C. What do you notice about the number of rods in C?

b) Is there only one way to make this lining up happen?

c) What fraction of a whole length of C would be equal to two parts of A plus one part of B?

Challenge 2: Sara has three identical lengths, A, B and C, as shown below. C is made up of 21 identical rods and the diagram shows $\frac{13}{21}$ of its length shaded. A and B are also made up of different sets of identical rods. The rods in A and B are not the same length as each other, nor the same length as the 21 rods that make C.

Sara can add together different numbers of rods from A and B to make different fractions of C.

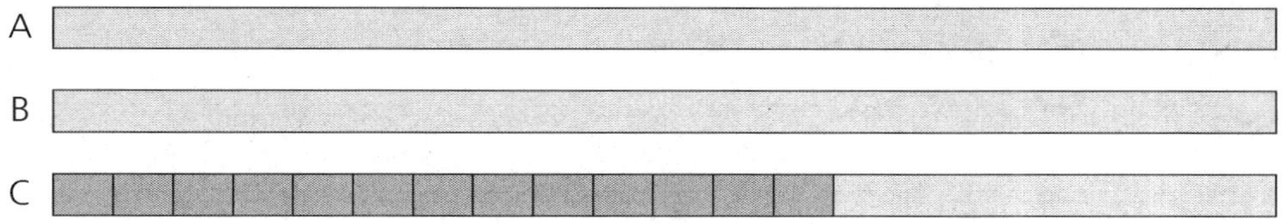

a) How many rods make up A and how many make up B?

b) Is it possible to calculate the fraction of A plus the fraction of B that are equal to $\frac{13}{21}$ of C?

c) What is the smallest number of rods in total that can be used to make up A and B?

Challenge 3: Preeti says that every fraction in its simplest form has prime numbers as the numerator and denominator. She is not quite right. Explain why she is wrong. Make a statement that improves on what Preeti thought.

Challenge 4: Which one of the following fractions is different to the others and why?

$$\frac{3}{7} \qquad \frac{15}{24} \qquad \frac{11}{7} \qquad \frac{25}{40} \qquad 1\frac{4}{7} \qquad \frac{5}{14} \qquad \frac{21}{49}$$

- *use common factors to simplify fractions; use common multiples to express fractions in the same denomination*

Challenge 1 Answer

a) There are five equal rods in A and three equal rods in B. 5 × 3 = 15, which is how many rods there are in C.

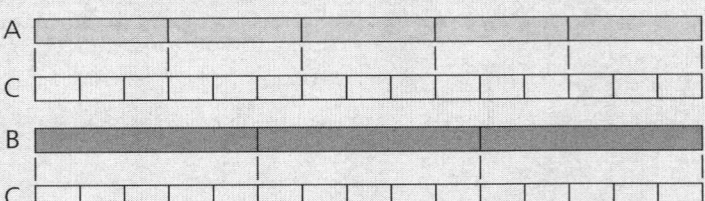

b) No, there are many more ways, but the rods in C would become smaller. For example, 30 would work because both 3 and 5 are factors of 30.

c) Two parts of A is $\frac{2}{5}$, which is equal to $\frac{6}{15}$ of the whole of C. One part of B is $\frac{1}{3}$, which is equal to $\frac{5}{15}$ of C. So two parts of A plus one part of B is $\frac{11}{15}$ of C.

Assessment

Check that pupils make an initial link to equivalent fractions in (a). They will know that length C is made of identical rods which are different to those in A and B. They should be able to find the smallest multiple of both 3 and 5 (15) and use this number for the number of rods in C.

In part (b), check that pupils do not insist that this solution of 15 equal rods is the only solution – there are an infinite number of possibilities, all multiples of 15; however, they could insist that 15 is the smallest possible solution.

In part (c), they are being asked to add two fractions with different denominators. They should use the result of (b) to inform their calculation process. Check that they convert the implied fractions in the question ($\frac{2}{5} = \frac{6}{15}$ and $\frac{1}{3} = \frac{5}{15}$) and add them to give the result $\frac{11}{15}$. Check they believe that the question is another way of solving the calculation $\frac{2}{5} + \frac{1}{3}$.

Challenge 2 Answer

a) Lengths A and B are made up of three and seven rods.

b) Yes it is possible: $\frac{2}{7}$ of A plus $\frac{1}{3}$ of B (or vice versa) is equal to $\frac{13}{21}$ of C.

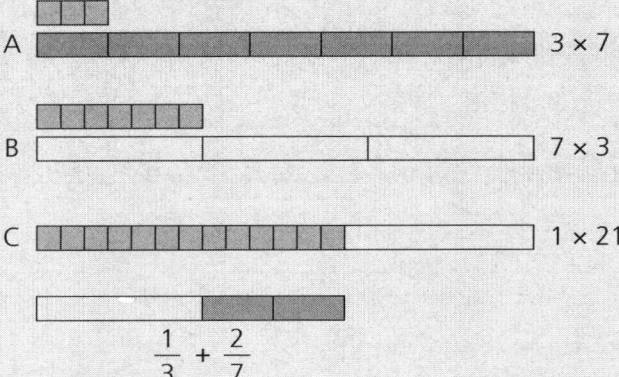

c) The smallest number of rods in total for A and B is 10 as sevenths and thirds are the smallest denominators that make a pair of factors of 21.

Assessment

Pupils are being asked to find a pair of factors of 21 in this challenge and may find the use of Cuisinaire rods, for example, useful.

In part (a), check that they have understood that the number of rods that make up A is a different number to both B and C and, as in Challenge 1, each end of a rod in both A and B must line up with an end of a rod in C.

Check that they have understood that finding factor pairs of 21 will help to solve the problem and that, as {1, 21} (21 rods of length 1) have already been used, {3, 7} (3 rods of length 7 and 7 rods of length 3) are the only pair left that will work.

Observe how they solve problem (b) once A and B are represented by 3 and 7 equal rods respectively. Are they using equipment to make sense of the problem and using trial and improvement to find that the solution to the problem is $\frac{1}{3}$ of A and $\frac{2}{7}$ of C?

Check that they are using a more fluent approach by finding combinations of multiples of 7 and 3 that total 13, and that they reason that 7 must be the only possibility in the multiples of 7 as all the others are greater than 13.

multiples of 3	3, ⑥ 9, 12, 15, 18...
multiples of 7	⑦ 14, 21, 28, 35...
Sum to 13	$7 + 6 = (7 \times \mathbf{1}) + (3 \times \mathbf{2})$

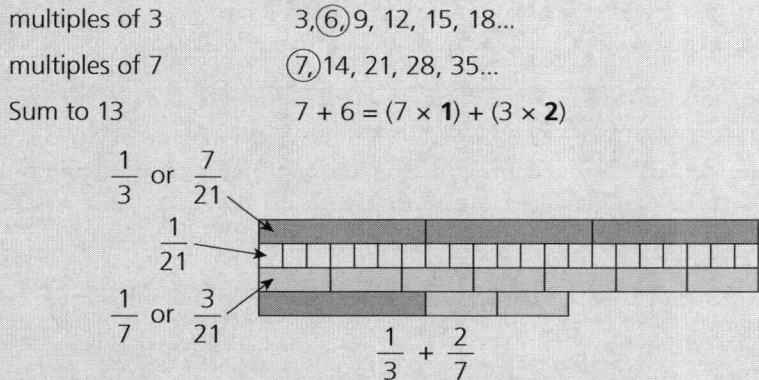

Challenge 3 Answer

Fractions do not have to have prime numbers for both numerator and denominator to be in their simplest form, but at least one of them must be an odd number. If a fraction has two even numbers, it can be simplified further by dividing both by 2. If a fraction has two different odd numbers, a further odd number could exist that would be a factor of both numerator and denominator, but often two odd numbers have no common factors. If the fraction consisted of two primes, it would be in its simplest form, as the only common factor would be 1 which is trivial and not a prime number.

Preeti could have said: 'For a fraction to be in its simplest form there must be at least one odd number in the fraction, be it numerator or denominator.'

Assessment

Check that pupils can reason that a prime number is not a necessity in a fraction in its simplest form, but that the denominator and numerator must either be an odd and an even number (for example $\frac{9}{14}$) or two odd numbers without a common factor such as $\frac{33}{35}$.

They should be able to give examples to back up their statements. Having given examples of fractions that are in their simplest form (as above) but which do not contain at least one prime, they should redefine Preeti's statement. They might suggest that a fraction in its simplest form can be defined as one where the numbers used for the denominator and numerator have no common factors. The following examples illustrate this definition: $\frac{16}{21}$, $\frac{35}{44}$, $\frac{9}{10}$ and $\frac{21}{55}$.

Challenge 4 Answer

Answers may vary; sample answer: $\frac{5}{14}$ because all the others are part of an equivalent pair.

Assessment

Check that pupils can convert between mixed numbers and improper fractions.

Having converted mixed numbers to improper fractions, check that they independently reduce all fractions to their lowest terms. They might use a table to sort these fractions, but it is not essential.

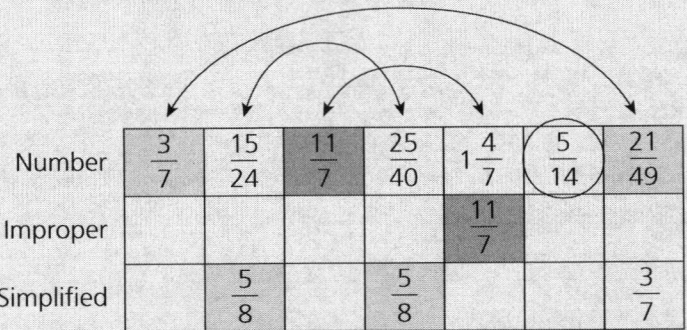

Number	$\frac{3}{7}$	$\frac{15}{24}$	$\frac{11}{7}$	$\frac{25}{40}$	$1\frac{4}{7}$	$\frac{5}{14}$	$\frac{21}{49}$
Improper					$\frac{11}{7}$		
Simplified		$\frac{5}{8}$		$\frac{5}{8}$			$\frac{3}{7}$

Some pupils will suggest that the odd number out is $1\frac{4}{7}$ as this is a mixed number and the others are proper and improper fractions. This answer is acceptable if accompanied by this reason, however the question is designed to get pupils to remark on the equality of pairs of numbers and, as such, is aimed at the answer that $\frac{5}{14}$ is the unique number.

Ask pupils who suggest $1\frac{4}{7}$ as the odd number if they think it is possible there is another answer.

Comparing, adding and subtracting

Challenge 5: Place the following fractions and mixed numbers in the correct order on a number line. Explain how you did this.

$$\boxed{\frac{9}{5}} \quad \boxed{\frac{5}{4}} \quad \boxed{\frac{19}{60}} \quad \boxed{1\frac{2}{3}} \quad \boxed{\frac{4}{5}} \quad \boxed{2\frac{7}{60}}$$

Challenge 6: Roddy has drawn a graph that he says shows which of two fractions is greater. He says that the darker line from P down to the bottom of the graph shows that $\frac{3}{3}$ and $\frac{9}{9}$ are equivalent.

He says that the second line shows that $\frac{2}{3}$ is greater than $\frac{5}{9}$.

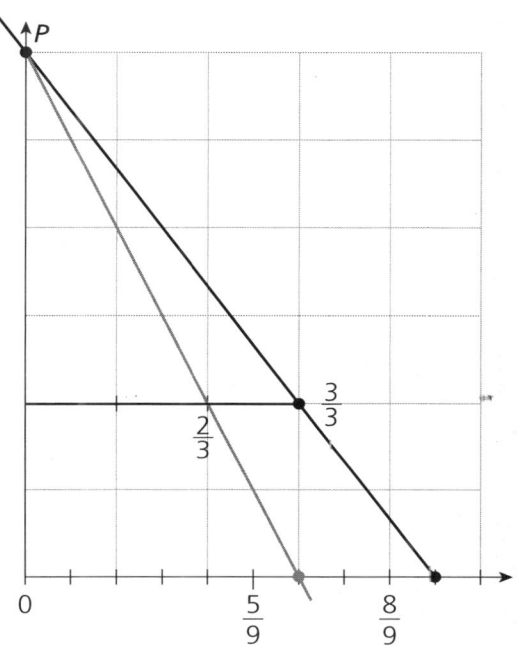

a) Do you agree that the graph shows that $\frac{2}{3}$ is greater than $\frac{5}{9}$?

b) Use Roddy's method to say which is the greater of $\frac{2}{3}$ and $\frac{3}{5}$ and explain why this graph will work with any two fractions. Demonstrate your thinking on squared or graph paper.

Challenge 7: What is the same and what is different about the following calculations?

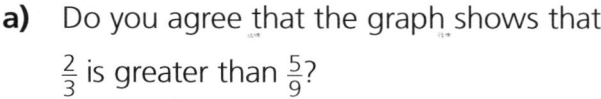

$$\boxed{\frac{3}{8} + \frac{7}{12}} \qquad \boxed{\frac{9}{24} + \frac{14}{24}} \qquad \boxed{\frac{46}{48} + \frac{21}{36}}$$

Challenge 8: The masses of three bags of potatoes must be added to work out the total mass of the potatoes.

The mass of bag A is $3\frac{3}{4}$ kg, B is $\frac{2}{3}$ kg lighter than A, and C is $1\frac{1}{4}$ kg heavier than B.

What is the total mass of the three bags?

National Curriculum objectives, Year 6, Fractions (including decimals and percentages)

- *compare and order fractions, including fractions > 1*
- *add and subtract fractions with different denominators and mixed numbers, using the concept of equivalent fractions*

Challenge 5 Answer

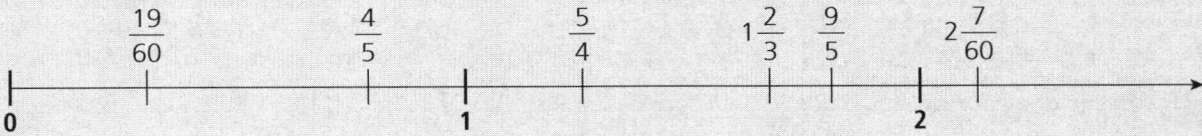

Assessment

Check that pupils can convert mixed numbers to improper fractions and then find the lowest common multiple of all the denominators (60) and convert all the fractions so they have equal denominators.

When this operation is complete, make sure that they are considering the numerators only when ordering them.

Once they have ordered all the fractions, do they convert them back to their original form and arrange them on a number line?

Challenge 6 Answer

a) Pupils should agree that the graph does show that $\frac{2}{3}$ is greater than $\frac{5}{9}$. The line through $\frac{2}{3}$ meets the longer line at $\frac{6}{9}$, which is further to the right than $\frac{5}{9}$.

b)

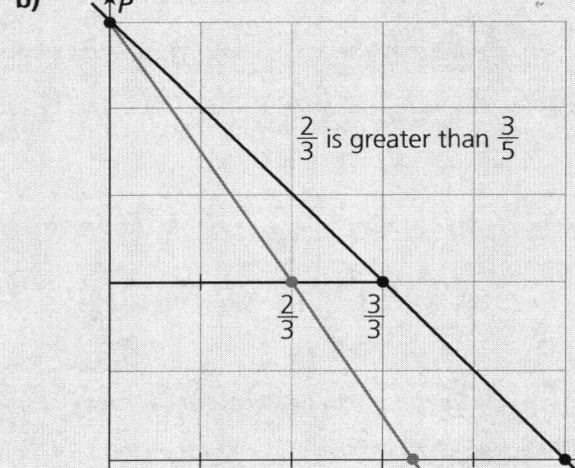

Assessment

Assess the pupils' ability to make sense of the graph. Do they notice that $\frac{2}{3}$ pairs with $\frac{6}{9}$ and that these fractions are equivalent? You could ask them to predict where a line going through $\frac{1}{3}$ would be on the line with ninths ($\frac{3}{9}$).

Pupils should agree with the statement in (a). They should be able to explain that the line from P crosses the bottom line at $\frac{6}{9}$, which is equal to $\frac{2}{3}$ and, as this line crosses to the right of $\frac{5}{9}$, $\frac{2}{3}$ must be the greater number.

In (b), check that they have constructed a graph modelled on the one in the example ƒand have arrived at the conclusion that $\frac{3}{5}$ is less than $\frac{2}{3}$. The most straightforward way to draw the graph would be to begin by drawing a vertical axis with P at the top. They then need to draw their thirds line covering three squares and below this a line covering five squares for fifths. They then draw a diagonal line from P through $\frac{3}{3}$ and $\frac{5}{5}$. When they then draw the diagonal line through $\frac{2}{3}$ it will cross the fifths line part-way between $\frac{3}{5}$ and $\frac{4}{5}$.

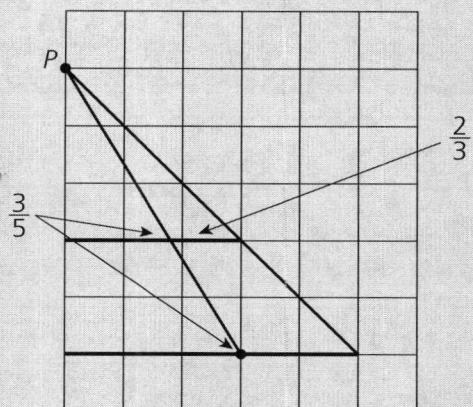

Ask them to do the same with $\frac{5}{8}$ and $\frac{4}{7}$, then with $\frac{7}{10}$ and $\frac{8}{11}$ and get them to make a conjecture about a second fraction with numerators and denominators that are one more than in the first fraction. They should suggest that the fraction with the smaller denominator is the smaller of the two. Get them to check by using equivalent fractions with identical denominators.

Assess their explanation as to why they can always compare fractions using this method. If they can explain confidently and with some examples, they are showing depth of understanding.

Challenge 7 Answer

There are various ways in which these calculations are the same, for example, they all have even denominators. The key similarity that pupils should identify is that the second fraction in each calculation is the same – they are all equivalent to $\frac{7}{12}$. There is a similarity between the first two in that both fractions are equivalent, so the answers will be the same.

There are several differences, for example, the third calculation has a different answer to the first two. The key difference is that the first calculation is the only one where the fractions are written in their simplest terms. Another difference is that only the second one can be calculated as it is – the others will need to be changed to fractions with the same denominator.

Assessment

Check that pupils can find common denominators and convert the fractions, simplifying when necessary. From this they will be able to see that the same element in all three expressions is the fraction $\frac{7}{12}$.

When they have converted the fractions, check that they can calculate the results and tell you that the answers to the first two are the same ($\frac{23}{24}$) and the third one is different ($\frac{9}{24}$ or $\frac{3}{8}$).

This challenge aims to bring out an understanding of the need for common denominators when adding or subtracting fractions and the usefulness and effectiveness of reducing fractions to their simplest form. Check that pupils are able to solve the following exercise: $\frac{15}{40} + \frac{9}{16}$. Look for an initial simplification of the first fraction followed by a manipulation of it, creating a common denominator of 16.

Challenge 8 Answer

$11\frac{1}{6}$ kg

Assessment

Check that pupils know that to find the mass of the second bag they need to take $\frac{2}{3}$ away from $3\frac{3}{4}$. This can be done by rewriting A as an improper fraction and converting the denominators of both A and B to 12:

$3\frac{3}{4} - \frac{2}{3}$ is equal to $\frac{15}{4} - \frac{2}{3}$, which is equal to $\frac{45}{12} - \frac{8}{12} = \frac{37}{12}$.

They would then convert the result to $3\frac{1}{12}$ kg to find the mass of B.

A similar process can be used to find the mass of C by adding $1\frac{1}{4}$ to $3\frac{1}{12}$:

$1\frac{3}{12} + 3\frac{1}{12} = 4\frac{4}{12}$ or $4\frac{1}{3}$ kg.

Pupils need to add all three masses ($3\frac{3}{4} + 3\frac{1}{12} + 4\frac{1}{3}$), arriving at the total mass of $11\frac{1}{6}$ kg.

Converting to improper fractions followed by converting to common denominators before calculation demonstrates good levels of fluency.

Does multiplication always give a greater value?

Challenge 9: Look at the following array which shows that $\frac{1}{4} \times \frac{1}{2} = \frac{1}{8}$.

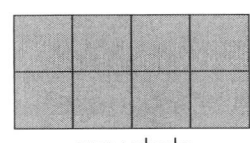 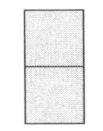  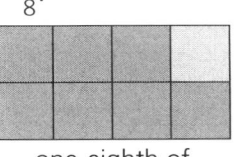

one whole   a quarter of   a half of   one-eighth of
              one whole   one-quarter   a whole
                            of a whole

a) Why do you think the array is a 4 × 2 rectangle?

b) Using the same idea, show that $\frac{1}{3} \times \frac{1}{2} = \frac{1}{6}$.

c) Using the same idea, show that $\frac{1}{2} \times \frac{1}{3} = \frac{1}{6}$.

Challenge 10: Use the method in the previous challenge to show the result of $\frac{2}{3} \times \frac{1}{5}$.

What do you think the mathematical operation is that gets the result?

Test your conjecture when finding the result of $\frac{3}{7} \times \frac{2}{3}$.

Julia thinks the result of $\frac{3}{3} \times \frac{2}{7}$ is the same as $\frac{3}{7} \times \frac{2}{3}$. Do you agree?

Challenge 11: In challenge 1 you were asked to make arrays that showed the results of fraction multiplication. Do the same with the following problem. It will not show the result in its simplest form.

$\frac{4}{5} \times \frac{1}{6}$

Using what you know about equivalent fractions, how can the multiplication be rearranged in order that the result is given in its simplest form immediately?

Challenge 12: Use a method of your choice to solve the following fraction problems. Show your working.

a) $\frac{3}{8} \times \frac{4}{9}$

b) $\frac{2}{11} \times \frac{5}{8}$

c) $\frac{6}{7} \times \frac{14}{15}$

Challenge 9 Answer

a) The numbers in the array (4 and 2) come from the denominators in the operation. These numbers allow us to see the whole in quarters and halves.

b)

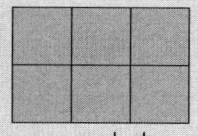

one whole

a third of one whole

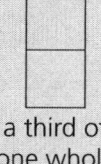

a half of one-third of a whole

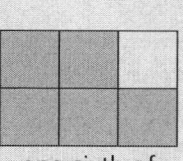

one-sixth of a whole

c)

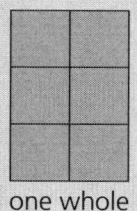

one whole

a half of one whole

a third of one-half of a whole

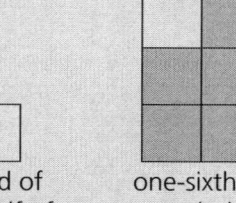

one-sixth of a whole

Assessment

In part (a), be clear that pupils have associated the 4 × 2 array with the possibility of a connection to the denominators of the fractions $\frac{1}{4}$ and $\frac{1}{2}$. They can be asked at this point why the connection might exist. Look for them explaining that a 4 × 2 array can easily be separated into quarters (columns) and halves (rows).

In part (b), look for them using the same logic and constructing a 3 × 2 array and confirming that this structure allows thirds and halves to be identified.

Part (c) is aimed at getting pupils to see that the commutative property in multiplication exists with fractions also. Make sure they have understood this by asking them if $\frac{9}{17} \times \frac{11}{19} = \frac{11}{19} \times \frac{9}{17}$ is a true statement. There should be no need at this point for them to give a result to both multiplications. They should use their knowledge of commutativity of multiplication without doing any calculation.

Challenge 10 Answer

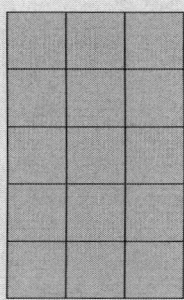

1

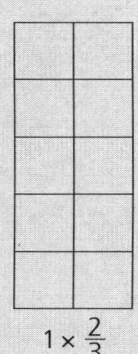

$1 \times \frac{2}{3}$

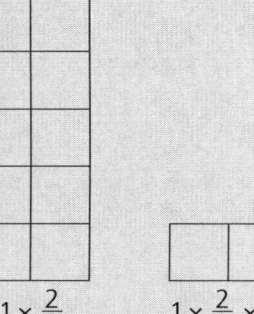

$1 \times \frac{2}{3} \times \frac{1}{5}$

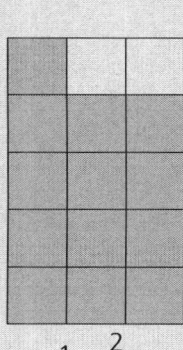

$1 \times \frac{2}{15}$

If the numerators are multiplied, then the denominators are also multiplied and the results of these operations are the numerator and denominator of the solution.

$$\frac{3}{7} \times \frac{2}{3} = \frac{3 \times 2}{7 \times 3} = \frac{6}{21}$$

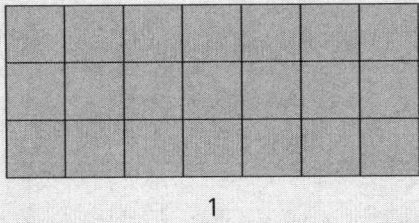 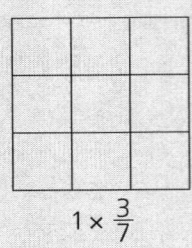 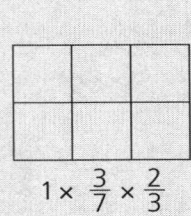 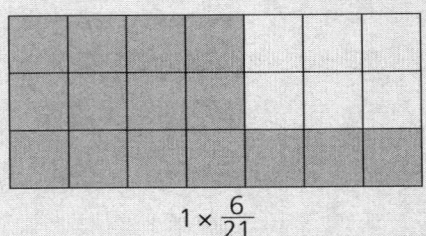

1   $1 \times \frac{3}{7}$ $1 \times \frac{3}{7} \times \frac{2}{3}$ $1 \times \frac{6}{21}$

Yes, $\frac{6}{21} = \frac{3}{7}$ so $\frac{3}{3} \times \frac{2}{7}$ is the same as $\frac{3}{7} \times \frac{2}{3}$.

Assessment

Check that pupils draw a 3 × 5 array to show that the result of $\frac{2}{3} \times \frac{1}{5}$ is $\frac{2}{15}$.

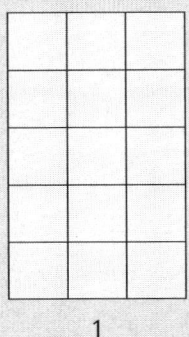 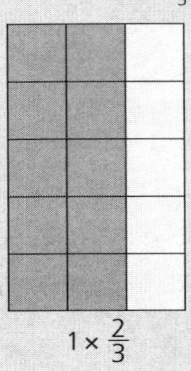 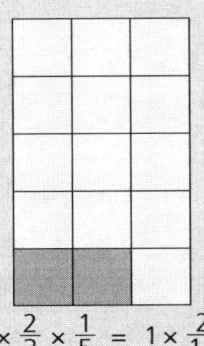

1   $1 \times \frac{2}{3}$ $1 \times \frac{2}{3} \times \frac{1}{5} = 1 \times \frac{2}{15}$

They should make the conjecture that both numerators and denominators are multiplied in order to calculate the result. Check that they use their conjecture on the multiplication $\frac{3}{7} \times \frac{2}{3}$ to get the result $\frac{6}{21}$ and that they follow up with a diagram of the calculation.

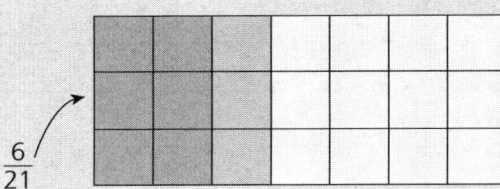

Finally, when they comment on Julia's conjecture, look for them to agree with her and to produce two diagrams that show the same result.

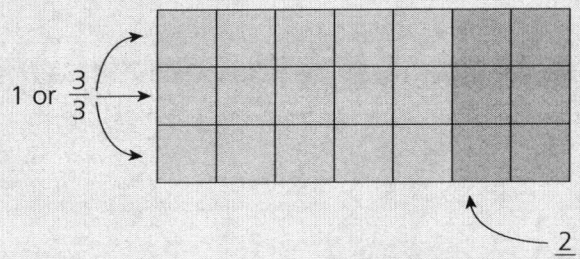 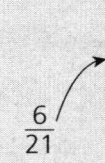 

Follow this up by asking them to decide if the following statement is true: $\frac{5}{8} \times \frac{7}{10} = \frac{5}{10} \times \frac{7}{8}$. If so, do they think it is always possible to exchange either numerators or denominators in a multiplication? Ask them why this is a useful fact in calculation. (In this example, $\frac{5}{8} \times \frac{7}{10} = \frac{5}{10} \times \frac{7}{8} = \frac{1}{2} \times \frac{7}{8}$, which without too much effort can be completed mentally to get the result $\frac{7}{16}$.)

Challenge 11 Answer

$\frac{4}{5} \times \frac{1}{6} = \frac{4}{30}$

Below is the array for $\frac{4}{5} \times \frac{1}{6}$.

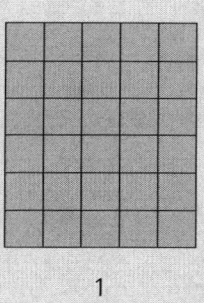  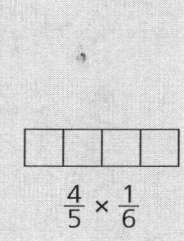 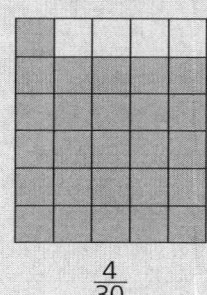

1 $\qquad$ $\frac{4}{5}$ $\qquad$ $\frac{4}{5} \times \frac{1}{6}$ $\qquad$ $\frac{4}{30}$

Convert the problem to $\frac{1}{5} \times \frac{4}{6}$ and rewrite $\frac{4}{6}$ as its equivalent fraction $\frac{2}{3}$, then the problem to be solved becomes $\frac{1}{5} \times \frac{2}{3}$.

Below is the array for $\frac{1}{5} \times \frac{2}{3}$.

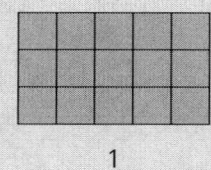 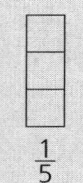 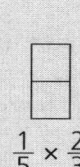 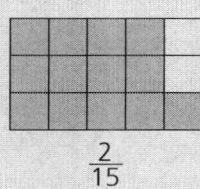

1 $\qquad$ $\frac{1}{5}$ $\quad$ $\frac{1}{5} \times \frac{2}{3}$ $\qquad$ $\frac{2}{15}$

Assessment

Check for fluency of application when pupils rearrange the problem and then simplify it to $\frac{1}{5} \times \frac{4}{6} = \frac{1}{5} \times \frac{2}{3}$.

They now have to show whether the statement $\frac{4}{5} \times \frac{1}{6} = \frac{1}{5} \times \frac{2}{3}$ is true or false.

Look for mental calculation of this problem using what they know about multiplication of numerators followed by multiplication of denominators ($\frac{4}{30}$ and $\frac{2}{15}$), which they could prove were equal with knowledge of equivalent fractions.

If they have not already provided it, ask them to show in diagram form how the result is the same if you simply complete the multiplication of the fraction given in the challenge.

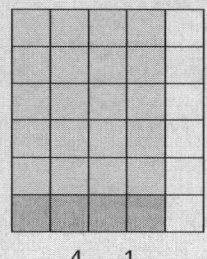 $\qquad$

$\frac{4}{5} \times \frac{1}{6}$ $\qquad\qquad$ $\frac{1}{5} \times \frac{2}{3}$

$\boxed{} = \boxed{} \times 2$

Challenge 12 Answer

a) $\quad \frac{3}{8} \times \frac{4}{9} = \frac{3}{9} \times \frac{4}{8} = \frac{1}{3} \times \frac{1}{2} = \frac{1}{6}$ $\qquad$ b) $\quad \frac{2}{11} \times \frac{5}{8} = \frac{2}{8} \times \frac{5}{11} = \frac{1}{4} \times \frac{5}{11} = \frac{5}{44}$ $\qquad$ c) $\quad \frac{6}{7} \times \frac{14}{15} = \frac{6}{15} \times \frac{14}{7} = \frac{2}{5} \times \frac{2}{1} = \frac{4}{5}$

Assessment

By this stage, pupils should be fluent with the process of multiplying fractions. In (a) they might rearrange the problem to $\frac{4}{8} \times \frac{3}{9}$ and simplify to $\frac{1}{2} \times \frac{1}{3}$, which can easily be calculated mentally.

In (b) they might rearrange to $\frac{2}{8} \times \frac{5}{11}$ and simplify to $\frac{1}{4} \times \frac{5}{11}$ and then multiply appropriately using a mental calculation.

Part (c) should see the pupils fluently rearranging the problem to $\frac{14}{7} \times \frac{6}{15}$ and simplifying to $2 \times \frac{2}{5}$, which is relatively easy to solve mentally.

Division of fractions

Challenge 13: Make an array and identify $\frac{1}{3}$ of it. Divide this by 2.

What fraction of the original whole array is this worth? You will need to use what you know about arrays when multiplying fractions to decide on the base and height of your chosen array.

What can you say about dividing a fraction by 2?

Can you predict what dividing $\frac{1}{3}$ by 3 would be?

Try a different but similar problem to check any thoughts you may have about what is happening.

Challenge 14: Use any method to solve the following division of fractions problems.

a) $\frac{2}{3} \div 2$

b) $\frac{2}{3} \div 4$

c) $\frac{3}{4} \div 5$

Challenge 15: Strips of wooden cladding are sold in $\frac{7}{8}$ m lengths.

a) If each strip of cladding is cut into five equal pieces, how long would each piece be? Give your answer as a fraction of one metre.

b) Without measuring or calculating, Glen says there is an exact number of strips that can be bought if he wanted to cut 24 of the small pieces without any wood being left over. He says this must be true because 8 in the fraction $\frac{7}{8}$ is a factor of 24.

Do you agree?

Challenge 16: Mrs Evans says that what applies to fractions also applies to whole numbers. She also says that if $\frac{4}{5} \div 3$ is equal to $\frac{4}{5} \times \frac{1}{3}$ then it is true that 12×4 is the same as $12 \div \frac{1}{4}$.

Ricky is not convinced. He says that when you divide a number by another it always produces a smaller number.

Who do you agree with and why?

- *divide proper fractions by whole numbers [for example $\frac{1}{3} \div 2 = \frac{1}{6}$]*

Challenge 13 Answer

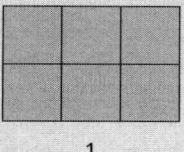

1            $1 \times \frac{1}{3}$ $1 \times \frac{1}{3} \div 2$ 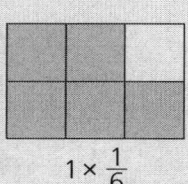 $1 \times \frac{1}{6}$

The effect of dividing by 2 is the same as multiplying by $\frac{1}{2}$. Dividing a fraction by 3 would be the same as multiplying it by $\frac{1}{3}$, so $\frac{1}{3} \div 3 = \frac{1}{9}$.

Assessment

Pupils might be expected to construct an array linking on from their understanding of multiplication of fractions. Check that they have considered the denominator in $\frac{1}{3}$ and the 2 that is used for the division. Look for them to use a 2×3 or 3×2 array.

Check that they can convince you that dividing a fraction by 2 gives the same result as multiplying it by $\frac{1}{2}$.

3 × 2 array

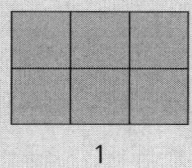 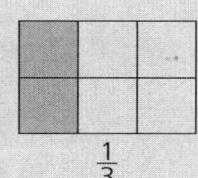 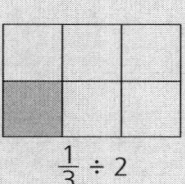

1                              $\frac{1}{3}$ $\frac{1}{3} \div 2$

Check that pupils are able to explain that division by 2 is the same as multiplication by its reciprocal ($\frac{1}{2}$) and encourage them to make further conjectures based on different fractions divided by other whole numbers.

Look for pupils making predictions about $\frac{1}{3} \div 3$ based on what they have just completed. They should be able to confidently state that the result is $\frac{1}{9}$ and show this in a diagram.

3 × 3 array

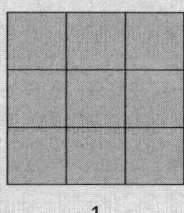 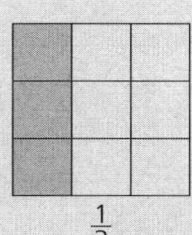 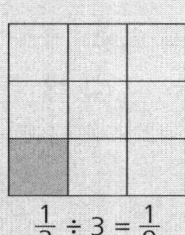

1                              $\frac{1}{3}$ $\frac{1}{3} \div 3 = \frac{1}{9}$

Ask pupils how they would calculate $\frac{2}{7} \div 2$ on paper without the use of a diagram.

Challenge 14 Answer

a)   This can be answered using mental methods. If you start with $\frac{2}{3}$ of something and then divide this into two equal parts you have $\frac{1}{3}$ of what you started with.

b) $\frac{1}{6}$

c) $\frac{3}{20}$

Assessment

Pupils may use a variety of strategies to solve these questions. In (a), for example, they could see this as two identical fractions ($\frac{1}{3} \times 2$). Logically, as this 'group' of two things (in this case the fraction 'one-third') is being divided by 2, the result is just one of them ($\frac{1}{3}$). This is not the only way to the solution, but it is very efficient and demonstrates that when a fraction is divided by a whole number, it is the numerator that is subject to the actual division. Pupils can be asked to comment on this conjecture to see if they agree.

In general, it would be useful for pupils to continue to make links to their growing knowledge of multiplication.

In (b), look for pupils who are systematically converting the problem to $\frac{2}{3} \times \frac{1}{4}$ and perhaps rearranging for a mental solution ($\frac{1}{3} \times \frac{2}{4} = \frac{1}{3} \times \frac{1}{2} = \frac{1}{6}$).

In (c), a straightforward conversion to multiplication ($\frac{3}{4} \times \frac{1}{5}$) should get to a mentally derived result of $\frac{3}{20}$. Pupils who are fluently rearranging the problems and solving mentally where possible are showing a high level of mastery at this stage.

Challenge 15 Answer

a)   The lengths of the pieces would be found through $\frac{7}{8} \div 5$ or better $\frac{7}{8} \times \frac{1}{5} = \frac{7}{40}$ m.

b)   Glen is wrong as each piece contains 5 equal lengths and 5 is not a factor of 24.

Assessment

Check that pupils understand that this question is similar to the previous challenge in which they were asked to divide a fraction by a whole number. In this case, the division is $\frac{7}{8}$ by 5, which they should be able to calculate by multiplying the fraction by the inverse of 5 ($\frac{7}{8} \times \frac{1}{5} = \frac{7}{40}$).

Pupils might approach (b) by multiplying $\frac{7}{40}$ by 24 and continuing the calculation from there. However, look for pupils who understand that it is not the 8 in the fraction that is important but the number of strips (five) and as 5 is not a factor of 24 then Glen's statement cannot be true.

Pupils could be asked to calculate the exact amount of cladding that would be needed for nine strips, allowing them to link multiplication of fractions by whole numbers.

Challenge 16 Answer

Mrs Evans is correct.

Assessment

Check that pupils are convinced that multiplication does not always result in a larger number than the numbers in the multiplication. Pupils at this stage will show acceptable levels of fluency by checking $12 \div \frac{1}{4}$, possibly with mathematics equipment.

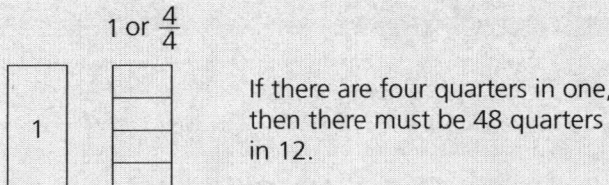

1 or $\frac{4}{4}$

If there are four quarters in one, then there must be 48 quarters in 12.

The approach in the diagram above would seem to be true for this particular problem, but it is worth checking that pupils can use this information to answer problems like $9 \div \frac{1}{3}$ – is it the same result as 9×3?

Check that pupils fully understand that the inverse process in calculations involving fractions with whole numbers and other fractions works in two ways:

- division by a number can become multiplication by the reciprocal of the same number
- multiplication of a number can become division by the reciprocal of the same number.

Number – Fractions (including decimals and percentages)

Multiplying and dividing fractions

Challenge 17: Using formal division methods, convert the following fractions into their decimal equivalents.

    a) $\frac{3}{4}$ **b)** $\frac{7}{8}$ **c)** $2\frac{3}{8}$ **d)** $\frac{5}{6}$ (give your answer to three decimal places)

Challenge 18: Look at the following number: **2503.71**.

    a) Write the value of every digit that it is made from.

    b) Multiply the number by:

        i) 10   **ii)** 1000   **iii)** 200

    c) Divide the number by:

        i) 10   **ii)** 90

    d) Here is a different number: **3.04**.

        Multiply it by: **i)** 7   **ii)** 11   **iii)** 21

Challenge 19: George and Mona each had a 1.5m length of wood.

George was asked to cut a piece $\frac{1}{5}$m long from his length of wood, plus another unknown length.

Mona was asked to cut a piece $\frac{3}{20}$m long and another unknown length.

After cutting their two lengths, they each had 0.65m of wood left from their original 1.5m piece.

Calculate the unknown lengths and write as fractions of a metre in their simplest form.

Challenge 20: $\frac{2}{3}$ of a roll of carpet covers 42.4m² of floor.

    a) How many square metres of carpet are there on a roll of carpet?

    b) How many square metres of carpet on seven rolls?

Challenge 17 Answer

a) 0.75   **b)** 0.875   **c)** 2.375   **d)** 0.833

Assessment

Check that pupils are using formal short division. Ask questions about what is happening when a digit is carried over to the place holder to the right to be clear that their understanding is sound.

$$0.75$$
$$4\,\overline{)3.^{3}0^{2}0}$$

"Why have you moved the 3 to this position?"

"4 does not divide 3 so I converted it to 30 tenths and I can divide 30 by 4."

It is essential that pupils understand the concept visually before formal written methods are used; this should enable them to explain why and how numbers are carried over to the next place holder after individual divisions.

In (d), check that they know that if a number is to be rounded to 3 decimal places then a calculation to 4 decimal places is necessary so that a decision on whether to round up or not can be made.

$$0.8333$$
$$6\,\overline{)5.^{5}0^{2}0^{2}0^{2}0}$$

"Why have you calculated to 4 decimal places?"

"The 4th place tells me whether the 3rd place should be left as it is or rounded up."

$$\frac{5}{6} = 0.833 \quad \text{(3 d.p.)}$$

Challenge 18 Answer

a) The values of the digits are: 2 (thousands), 5 (hundreds), 0 (tens), 3 (ones), 7 (tenths) and 1 (hundredth).

b) **i)** 25 037.1   **ii)** 2 503 710   **iii)** 500 742

c) **i)** 250.371   **ii)** 27.819

d) **i)** 21.28   **ii)** 33.44   **iii)** 63.84

Assessment

In (a), allow pupils to express the digit values in words or numbers or a mixture (for example, '2 means 2000' or, '2 represents two thousand' or 'the 2 in the number means 2 thousand') as we are assessing their understanding of the value of each digit in the number.

In (b i) and (b ii), check that pupils are not simply routinely following a learned procedure, but can explain why the results are what they are (for example, in (b i) 2503.71 × 10 means that every digit in the number becomes 10 times its value, so 3 becomes 30, 500 becomes 5000, etc.).

In (b iii), check that they can solve the problem by first multiplying by 2 then by 100; similarly with (c ii), make sure they first divide by 9 and then by 10.

In (d), observe how often the problems are dealt with using some form of mental strategy so that a formal written method can be avoided. For example:

$$3.04 \times 7 \quad \begin{array}{l} 3 \times 7 = 21 \\ + \\ 0.04 \times 7 = 0.28 \end{array} = 21.28$$

$$3.04 \times 21 \quad \begin{array}{l} (3.04 \times 2) \times 10 = (6.08) \times 10 = 60.8 \\ + \\ 3.04 \times 1 = 3.04 \end{array} = 63.84$$

$3.04 \times 21 \approx 3 \times 21 = 63$ Estimation first?

$$\begin{array}{r} 3\,0\,4 \\ \times\,2\,1 \\ \hline 6\,0\,8\,0 \\ 3\,0\,4 \\ \hline 6\,3\,8\,4 \end{array}$$

= 63.84

Decimal point must be placed so that the answer is as close to the estimate as possible.

Challenge 19 Answer

George's unknown piece measured $\frac{13}{20}$ m.

Mona's unknown piece measured $\frac{7}{10}$ m.

Assessment

Look out for the potential trap in this question – some pupils might find the fractions of the length of wood and not of a metre as asked for.

Do pupils first calculate how much wood is left after cutting the pieces that are given in the question? George is left with 1.3m or 130cm (150cm – 20cm) and Mona is left with 1.35m or 135cm (150cm – 15cm). Check the methods pupils used – mental solutions are not too difficult for these problems. Did they use advanced problem-solving skills by converting the length of the wood to centimetres or millimetres, thus giving whole numbers to work with?

To calculate the unknown lengths George and Mona cut, pupils should subtract 0.65m (or 65cm) from the answers they found in step 1. This will give George's unknown length as 65cm (130cm – 65cm = 65cm) and Mona's as 70cm (135cm – 65cm = 70cm). Finally, pupils need to convert these lengths to fractions of a metre in their simplest form: 65cm = $\frac{13}{20}$ m and 70cm = $\frac{7}{10}$ m.

Challenge 20 Answer

a)   63.6m²

b)   445.2m²

Assessment

Did pupils calculate a full roll of carpet by halving 42.4m² (to find a third) and then multiplying by 3 (21.2 × 3 = 63.6m²)? This is evidence of sound mathematical reasoning. This reasoning is vital with questions of this nature as year 6 pupils are not expected to formally multiply quantities by fractions like $\frac{2}{3}$ and certainly not, as in this case, to multiply 42.4 by the inverse of $\frac{2}{3}$ ($\frac{3}{2}$) to get to the answer of 63.6m² for the area of a full roll of carpet in one operation.

Check their methods of finding the solution to seven rolls of carpet. It will probably be necessary to use formal multiplication methods.

$63.6 \times 7 \approx 60 \times 7 = \textbf{420}$ Estimation first?

$$\begin{array}{r} 6\,3\,6 \\ \times\,7 \\ \hline 4\,2\,0\,0 \\ 2\,1\,0 \\ 4\,2 \\ \hline 4\,4\,5\,2 \end{array}$$

= 445.2

Decimal point must be placed so that the answer is as close to the estimate as possible.

Solving fractions problems

Challenge 21: a) Solve the following problems, giving your answer to two decimal places for each one.

    i) $72 \div 7$

    ii) $814 \div 6$

    iii) $19.5 \div 8$

b) The last electricity bill in Davina's house was £78.50 and she paid $\frac{5}{6}$ of it. How much did she actually pay?

Challenge 22:

If I save $\frac{1}{8}$ of my salary this month and 15% next month I will have saved $\frac{1}{4}$ of my monthly salary altogether.

Explain why Janine is either correct or incorrect.

Challenge 23: A pair of £45 shoes were bought in a sale with a $\frac{2}{5}$ reduction. Another pair labelled £124 were bought in a sale with a 17.5% reduction.

How much is the total saving on both pairs?

Challenge 24: a) Place the following numbers in order of size starting with the lowest.

0.95, 40%, $\frac{3}{5}$, 0.5, $\frac{13}{10}$, 115%

b) Jan says that he would rather have 95% of €40 than $\frac{2}{5}$ of €95. Which would you prefer?

National Curriculum objectives, Year 6, Fractions
(including decimals and percentages)

- *solve problems which require answers to be rounded to specified degrees of accuracy*
- *recall and use equivalences between simple fractions, decimals and percentages, including in different contexts*

Challenge 21 Answer

a)   **i)**   10.29   **ii)**   135.67   **iii)**   2.44

b)   Davina would pay £65.42 as this is the result rounded to two decimal places.

Assessment

Check that pupils are routinely estimating the result before calculation and checking that the completed calculation is close in value to the estimation ($72 \div 7 \approx 10$; $814 \div 6 \approx 800 \div 5 = 160$; $19.5 \div 8 \approx 2$). This will help them to be more confident when dealing with divisions resulting in decimals.

In (a), it is assumed that formal short division methods will be used and results checked against estimations, which will help pupils decide where decimal points should be placed. For example, for (a ii):

$$814 \div 6 \approx 800 \div 5 = \mathbf{160}$$

$$\begin{array}{r} 1\,3\,5\,6\,6\,6 \\ 6\,\overline{)8^2 1^3 4^4 0^4 0^4 0} \end{array}$$

After estimation the addition of as many zeros as necessary is possible as the placing of any decimal point needed will be suggested by the estimation itself.

$$= \mathbf{135.67} \quad (2 \text{ d.p.})$$

In (b), pupils should reason that if $\frac{1}{6}$ is found, then the remainder is what Davina paid. Some pupils might calculate $\frac{1}{6}$ of £78.50 then multiply this by 5, others might calculate $\frac{1}{6}$ and subtract this from the total bill. Again, estimation should be encouraged and acknowledged as part of the calculation process.

$$£78.50 \div 6 \approx \mathbf{13} \qquad\qquad £78.50 - £13.083$$

$$\begin{array}{r} 1\,3\,0\,8\,3\,3\,3 \\ 6\,\overline{)7^1 8^2 5^5 0^2 0^2 0^2 0} \end{array}$$

$$= \mathbf{13.083} \quad (3 \text{ d.p.})$$

$$\begin{array}{r} 9 \\ 4\;\cancel{10}\;10 \\ 7\,8\,.\,\cancel{5}\,0\,0 \\ -\,1\,3\,.\,0\,8\,3 \\ \hline 6\,5\,.\,4\,1\,7 \end{array}$$

$$= £\mathbf{65.42} \quad (2 \text{ d.p.})$$

Challenge 22 Answer

$\frac{1}{8} + \frac{15}{100} = \frac{110}{400} = \frac{11}{40}$ $\frac{11}{40} > \frac{1}{4}$, therefore she is incorrect.

Assessment

Pupils should realise that the lack of an amount of salary in the question is unimportant as the problem is a straightforward addition of fractions, followed by a comparison. Check that reasoning has been exhausted before calculations are entered into. Are pupils aware that $\frac{1}{8}$ is half of $\frac{1}{4}$? If so, do they believe that 15% is equivalent to $\frac{1}{8}$ because, if it is, then Janine must be correct? Reasoning should influence their understanding that a quarter of one month's salary is the same as an eighth of two months' salary.

Check that they have reasoned that rewriting the percentage and the fraction as decimals allows a comparison to be made.

Have they divided 1 by 8 to find the decimal equivalent of $\frac{1}{8}$ (0.125)?

Check that they know that 15% = $\frac{15}{100}$ = 0.15. Some pupils may wish to keep their working out in fraction form as both will achieve the same goal.

When decimal equivalents have been calculated for the saving each month, does their sum equal 0.25 ($\frac{1}{4}$ of a month's salary)? 0.15 + 0.125 = 0.275 so pupils will be able to assert that Janine is incorrect.

Challenge 23 Answer

Total saving is £18 on the first pair plus £21.70 on the second pair, a total of £39.70.

Assessment

Check that pupils can calculate $\frac{1}{5}$ of £45 by dividing by 5 and reason from this that $\frac{2}{5}$ must be double that and arrive at the saving as £9 × 2 = £18.

Check that pupils understand that 17.5% is the sum of 10%, 5% and 2.5%, which is a process of halving each consecutive percentage. Make sure they can calculate 10% of £124 = £12.40, 5% (half of this) is £6.20 and 2.5% (half of 5%) is £3.10 and then add these to get the total saving of £21.70.

Make sure they then add this to the saving from the first pair (£21.70 + £18 = £39.70).

Challenge 24 Answer

a) 40%, 0.5, $\frac{3}{5}$, 0.95, 115%, $\frac{13}{10}$

b) They are both equal to €38.

Assessment

Pupils should reason that (a) will be solved more easily if all the numbers are in the same format, either decimal, fraction or percentage. In this problem, the most efficient choice would be to convert to decimals. Ask pupils if they agree or whether they think percentages or fractions would be better.

Ask pupils if they made the equivalent fraction $\frac{6}{10}$ for the given $\frac{3}{5}$ to get to 0.6 or if they used a different method.

After converting, did they order the numbers and then convert back to the original format?

Check the methods of calculation used in (b) as a variety are available.

Pupils may have reasoned that 5% of €40 is €2 because 10% is €4 and calculated from this position that 95% is €38.

Look for pupils who can reason that if $\frac{1}{5}$ is twice the value of $\frac{1}{10}$ then $\frac{1}{5}$ of €95 is €9.50 × 2 (€19) and who can double this to find $\frac{2}{5}$ of €95 (€38). This takes pupils to the conclusion that Jan does not know that both amounts are the same.

Ratio and proportion

Fractions, ratio or both?

Challenge 1: Maria and Neil share £35 in the ratio 2:5.

How much more money does Neil have than Maria?

Challenge 2: Oliver and Petra walk a total of 42km each week to school. Oliver walks 24km.

What is the ratio of kilometres walked each week by the two pupils in its simplest form?

Challenge 3: Stefan decides to make a cake for 8 people. He uses 4 eggs, 200g flour, 200g sugar, 200g butter and 60g dark chocolate.

The following week he makes enough cake for 18 people.

How much of each ingredient does he need?

Challenge 4: The pie chart shows the results of a football team supporters' survey in a school. The percentage of pupils who support either Chelsea or Leicester City is 75%. The ratio of Chelsea to Leicester supporters is 7:8. 45 pupils support either Manchester United or Aston Villa.

a) How many pupils said they preferred Leicester City?

b) What fraction of those surveyed prefer Chelsea?

National Curriculum objectives, Year 6, Ratio and proportion

- *solve problems involving the relative sizes of two quantities where missing values can be found by using integer multiplication and division facts*
- *solve problems involving calculations of percentages [for example, of measures, and such as 15% of 360] and the use of percentages for comparisons*
- *solve problems involving similar shapes where the scale factor is known or can be found*
- *solve problems involving unequal sharing and grouping using knowledge of fractions and multiples*

Challenge 1 Answer

Neil has £15 more than Maria.

Assessment

Pupils should reason that £35 has effectively been split into 7 equal parts with Maria receiving 2 of those parts and Neil the remaining 5.

Check that pupils have divided £35 by 7 to find the value of one part (£5), which they then multiply by 2 for Maria's share (£10) and by 5 for Neil's share (£25).

Check also that pupils are routinely checking their results by adding the two sums given to Maria and Neil and checking that the answer is equal to £35. If pupils do not get a sum of £35, ask them whether they think their calculation is correct and, if not, where their mistake could have happened.

Ask pupils if they can see a link between this ratio problem and fractions. If they can, ask them what fractions appear in this problem (sevenths) and why this particular fraction appears.

Challenge 2 Answer

The ratio of kilometres walked is 4:3.

Assessment

Pupils should reason that it takes two people to walk the total of 42km and that one of them (Oliver) has walked 24km of the total, which means that Petra has walked the other 18km.

Check that pupils are starting to make further links to fractions by asking them what is represented by the 'whole' in this problem (42km).

Can pupils use the information given in the problem, together with their calculations, to calculate that of the total distance of 42km, Oliver has walked $\frac{24}{42}$ as a fraction of it and Petra has walked $\frac{18}{42}$?

Check that they can simplify these fractions to $\frac{4}{7}$ and $\frac{3}{7}$ respectively.

Check that pupils understand that the value of the 'whole' has changed from 42 to 7 and that the ratio of kilometres walked each week by the two pupils in its simplest form is 4:3.

Some pupils may start to take an algebraic approach to this type of problem by initially seeing the problem as an addition of two fractions with identical denominators, of which one numerator is unknown.

$\frac{24}{42} + \frac{n}{42} = \frac{42}{42} \Rightarrow 24 + n = 42$

From this, they calculate 18km as Petra's part of the total journey. They continue this idea by reducing both fractions to their simplest form. Once this is completed they know that the ratio of one to the other is simply the numerator values of the simplified fraction.

$\frac{24}{42} + \frac{18}{42} = \frac{12}{21} + \frac{9}{21} = \frac{4}{7} + \frac{3}{7} \Rightarrow 4:3$

Challenge 3 Answer

Stefan uses 9 eggs, 450g flour, 450g sugar, 450g butter and 135g dark chocolate.

Assessment

Pupils should reason that this ratio problem relies heavily on the connection to fractions.

They should reason that all of the original amounts and the number of people the cake is made for are divisible by 2 and that this will help them to find the amounts for a cake for 18 people (which is also divisible by 2). They should be able to see from the original information that it would be possible to make a cake for two people by dividing all the ingredient amounts by 4. If these numbers are then multiplied by 9 there will be enough cake for 18 people.

When pupils have found the ratio of ingredients for two people by dividing all by 4 they should simplify their results to:

eggs : flour : sugar : butter : chocolate :: 1 : 50g : 50g : 50g : 15g

Check for fluency – can pupils write the ratio for two people as e : f : s : b : c :: 1 : 50g : 50g : 50g : 15g?

Ask them whether they think the g is necessary on the right-hand side of the ratio. (Expect them to say that it is as the numbers written represent both grams and numbers of eggs.)

Can pupils now convert this to the quantity of ingredients needed for a cake for 18 people by multiplying the data by 9 (2 × 9 = 18) and arriving at the ratio e : f : s : b : c :: 9 : 450g : 450g : 450g : 135g?

Challenge 4 Answer

a)   72 pupils prefer Leicester City.

b) $\frac{63}{180} = \frac{7}{20}$

Assessment

Pupils should reason that the problem can be solved through fractions as well as percentages.

Can they state that because $\frac{3}{4}$ of those surveyed support Chelsea and Leicester City then the 45 pupils who voted for Manchester United and Aston Villa represent the other $\frac{1}{4}$?

Check that pupils can calculate the number of Chelsea and Leicester City supporters from this: 45 × 3 = 135 ($\frac{3}{4}$ of the vote).

Check that pupils are able to divide this figure (135) in the ratio C : L :: 7 : 8 by first dividing by 15 (7 + 8, the 'whole' in its simplest form), followed by a multiplication of the result by 7 and 8 (135 ÷ 15 = 9, therefore C : L :: (7 × 9) : (8 × 9) = 63 : 72).

Check that pupils cross-reference this result by adding the two totals and making 135.

Look out for potential traps in (b) as the question asks for the fraction of Chelsea supporters from the whole survey. Pupils should identify the number of Chelsea supporters as 63 and the total number of voters as 180 arriving at the fraction $\frac{63}{180}$, which is an acceptable answer.

Check that pupils are routinely simplifying fractions at this stage and give the answer to (b) as $\frac{7}{20}$.

Ratio and proportion

Ratio in parts

Challenge 5: You will need cubes and counters. You can exchange 3 cubes for 12 counters.

    a)   How many counters can you exchange for 8 cubes?

    b)   How many cubes can you exchange for 36 counters?

    c)   What is the difference between converting cubes to counters and counters to cubes?

    d)   Is it possible to convert 42 counters into cubes? If not, why not?

Challenge 6: A horse eats five times more hay than a goat each day.

    a)   What would it cost to feed a horse if it costs £1.80 to feed a goat?

    b)   If it costs £4 to feed a horse every day, how much will it cost to feed a goat?

    c)   If it costs £3.50 a day to feed a horse, what would be the total cost to feed three horses and five goats?

Challenge 7: Two shoppers have a combined total of £50 in their wallets. Shopper A has exactly £8 less in her wallet than shopper B.

    a)   How much is in each wallet?

    b)   What percentage of the total money does each shopper have?

    c)   If the amount in each wallet was different and shopper A had 75% of it, leaving shopper B with £32, how much would shopper A have?

Challenge 8: Anna has 12 more cards than Barry. Clare has twice as many cards as Anna. Altogether they have 92 cards. How many cards do they each have?

National Curriculum objectives, Year 6, Ratio and proportion

- *solve problems involving similar shapes where the scale factor is known or can be found*
- *solve problems involving unequal sharing and grouping using knowledge of fractions and multiples*

Challenge 5 Answer

a) 8 cubes are equivalent to 32 counters.

b) 36 counters are equivalent to 9 cubes.

c) To convert cubes to counters we multiply the number of cubes by 4. To convert counters to cubes we divide the number of counters by 4.

d) It is not possible to get an exact number of cubes because 42 is not divisible by 4.

Assessment

From the concrete model of 3 cubes being equal to 12 counters, pupils should be able to deduce that 1 cube is equal to 4 counters.

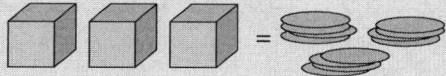 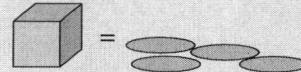

Importantly, the link to multiplication and division should be made. This will enable a more fluent approach of multiplying the number of cubes by 4 to calculate the equivalence in counters and using the inverse process to calculate the number of cubes from a given number of counters.

Pupils should reason from the concrete equipment they are given that one cube is equal to four counters and should be able to fluently calculate this from the information given (1 cube = 12 counters ÷ 3).

In (a), fluency of application of this simple algebraic understanding is being demonstrated if pupils multiply both sides of the equation by 8:

8 (1 cube) = 8 (12 counters ÷ 3) ⇒ 8 cubes = 32 counters.

A simple multiplication of 4 counters by 8 is acceptable from their understanding of the exchange.

Are pupils using the inverse process in (b) and dividing 36 by 4 to arrive at the result of 9 cubes?

It will be useful to discuss the question in (c) with pupils to see if they are able to explain that the operations are opposite to each other or, even better, that the operations are the inverse of each other.

In (d), look for their use of knowledge of tables to inform their answer as opposed to an actual calculation. They should be able to tell you that it is not possible to convert 42 counters into an exact number of cubes as 4 is not a factor of 42.

Challenge 6 Answer

a) £9 **b)** £0.80 **c)** £14

The bar method would be useful to help solve the particular type of ratio problem in (a).

| Goat ☐ = £1.80 |
| Horse ☐☐☐☐☐ = £9.00 |

Assessment

Check that pupils understand that (a) is a simple multiplication problem as a horse costs 5 times more than a goat (£1.80 × 5 = £9).

In (b), they are given the cost to feed a horse so expect pupils to divide this figure by 5 to calculate the cost of feeding one goat (£4 ÷ 5 = £0.80).

Question (c) requires more manipulation and gives an opportunity to assess mathematical fluency. Pupils should be expected to calculate the cost of feeding one goat first (£3.50 ÷ 5 = £0.70). They should then add the cost of the three horses (£3.50 × 3 = £10.50) and the cost of the five goats (£0.70 × 5 = £3.50), arriving at a total of £14. Check how many pupils were able to avoid the last multiplication by converting the cost of the five goats to one horse, leaving a simple multiplication: £3.50 × 4 = £14.

Challenge 7 Answer

a) Shopper A has £21 and shopper B has £29.

b) Shopper A has 42% and shopper B has 58%.

c) £96

Assessment

Pupils should reason that shoppers A and B would have an equal amount if the £8 difference was subtracted from the £50 (leaving £42) and this was divided by 2, leaving each with £21.

If they can reason this far, then they should be able to argue that by adding the £8 difference to shopper B (giving them £29), the sum of both shoppers' amounts is back at £50 and A does indeed have £8 less than B.

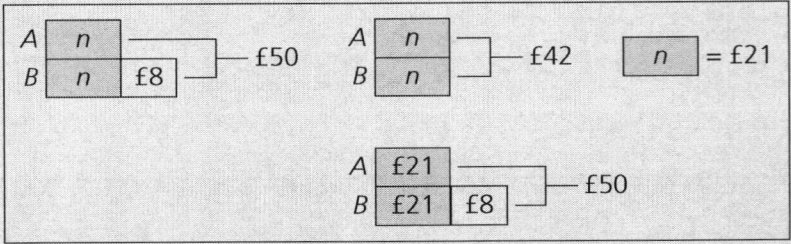

In (b) they should reason that as fractions, the ratio of shopper A : B is $\frac{21}{50} : \frac{29}{50} :: \frac{42}{100} : \frac{58}{100}$ and from this they should have calculated the percentages of A and B respectively as 42% and 58%.

In question (c), pupils should reason that 25% of the total amount is £32 and therefore 75% is 3 times this amount (£96). Ask pupils if it is an easier problem to solve by converting percentages to fractions first.

Challenge 8 Answer

Anna has 26 cards, Barry has 14 cards and Clare has 52 cards.

Assessment

Pupils should be clear that the important character in this problem is Barry as the other two can be constructed in both concrete and algebraic ways.

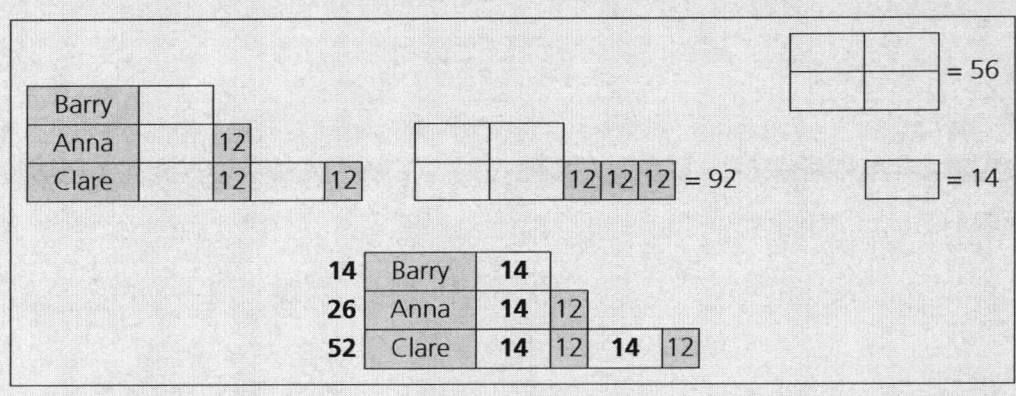

A more fluent approach is an algebraic one that states that if Barry has n cards then Anna has n + 12 and from that Clare has 2(n + 12) or 2n + 24 cards. The total is 92 cards and the equation 4n + 24 = 92 might be constructed by pupils with a greater mastery of year 6 algebra. By subtracting 36 from both sides of the equation we are left with 4n = 56 and a final division by 4 leaves n = 14, which is the number of cards that Barry owns and this figure can now be substituted into Anna's and Clare's equations (Anna = 14 + 12 = 26 and Clare = Anna × 2 = 52).

Solving this problem does not require a completely abstract approach through algebraic equations; a mixture of concrete apparatus and algebra may be seen.

Algebra

Pattern searching

Challenge 1: The first three patterns in a sequence are drawn below.

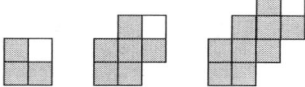

    a) What is the same about all three of them?

    b) How many squares would be in the fourth pattern?

    c) How many would be in the *n*th pattern?

    d) How many would be in the 50th pattern?

Challenge 2: Gianluca started a number sequence by doubling each number of the sequence position then adding 3. Mathilde started her number sequence by multiplying each number of the sequence position by 3 then adding 2.

    a) Write the first 10 terms of each of their number sequences and write the rule in terms of *t* (term) and *n* (position).

    b) What is the same about both number sequences and why do you think this happens? Explain a rule in words that results in the same number being generated in both sequences. For example, 5 is seen in both sequences, as are 11 and 17.

    c) The first two terms that appear in both number sequences are 5 and 11. Find the next three and give this new sequence a name in terms of *n* and *t*. What does this sequence generate?

Challenge 3: A yoga club has 23 members and has decided to take five new members each day for the next 30 days.

    a) How many days will pass before the club has 78 members?

    b) If the club always takes five new members each day, is it possible that it can ever have 84 members at the end of a day? Explain how you know you are right.

    c) How many days would pass before the club has 108 members?

Challenge 4: I have £43 in my bank account and every week my aunt puts in £7.

    a) Write a rule that allows me to work out how much money is in my account after any given number of weeks.

    b) How many weeks would pass before I have exactly £127 in my account?

National Curriculum objectives, Year 6, Algebra

- *use simple formulae*
- *generate and describe linear number sequences*
- *express missing number problems algebraically*
- *find pairs of numbers that satisfy an equation with two unknowns*
- *enumerate possibilities of combinations of two variables*

Challenge 1 Answer

a) They all have one white square at the top right. To the bottom left of these squares are groups of three L-shaped shaded squares.

b) 13 **c)** $3n + 1$ **d)** 151

Assessment

Pupils should see in (a) that each pattern has exactly one white square. Look for pupils who also notice that the shapes are made of an increasing number of 'L' arrays of grey squares.

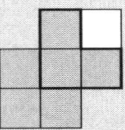

In (b), pupils who have recognised the 'L' growth in each consecutive pattern will be in a better position to define what is happening and work out how many squares would be in the fourth pattern. They might see that in the first shape there is one 'L' containing three squares plus the white square, in the second there are two 'L's plus one white square, the third has three Ls and one white square and so on. From this, they can see that the result for the fourth pattern would be $3 \times 4 + 1 = 13$. Check that pupils can turn the 'L' shape into a constant value of three squares so that it is so many threes plus the extra one white square each time.

In (c), pupils are demonstrating evidence of greater mastery and fluency of approach if they have recognised that the number of squares in the pattern is defined by n (number of 'L' shapes) plus one white square and can label the pattern as number of squares $= 3n + 1$ (n = position of the shape in the sequence).

In (d) it is not efficient for pupils to simply find a common difference in number of squares and to keep adding this difference until they get to the 50th pattern. Although this will get a correct result, it lacks the fluency of approach expected at year 6. A more efficient use of mathematics will be to substitute the value 50 for n in $3n + 1$.

Challenge 2 Answer

a) Gianluca = {5, 7, 9, 11, 13, 15, 17, 19, 21, 23}, Mathilde = {5, 8, 11, 14, 17, 20, 23, 26, 29, 32}

Gianluca's sequence is $t = 2n + 3$. Mathilde's sequence is $t = 3n + 2$.

b) Both sequences start with $t = 5$. There is a pattern where every consecutive third term after $t = 5$ in Gianluca's sequence is also seen in Mathilde's sequence. This can also be seen as every consecutive second term after $t = 5$ in Mathilde's sequence can be seen in Gianluca's. The diagrams explain what can be seen. The sentences in speech marks are what should be sought as a typical response to this question.

	n	1	2	3	4	5	6	n
Gianluca	t	5	7	9	11	13	15	$2n + 3$
Mathilde	t	5	8	11	14	17	20	$3n + 2$

"This is the rule that generates these numbers."

	n	1	4	7	10	13	n
Gianluca	t	5	11	17	23	29	2n + 3
Mathilde	t	5	11	17	23	29	3n + 2
	n	1	3	5	7	9	n

"If I start at the first term in Gianluca's sequence then leap forward three terms I get the same result as starting at the first term of Mathilde's then leaping forward two terms."

c) The next three terms that appear in both sequences are 17, 23 and 29. This can be expressed as $t = 6n - 1$. It tells us that each number in the sequence will be found in both Gianluca's and Mathilde's.

0	n	1	2	3	4	5	n
−1	t	5	11	17	23	29	6n − 1

+6

Assessment

Check that pupils are starting to organise the information into tables with values for both n and t as shown in the answers.

In (b), look for pupils who can explain that the first value of 5 is due to a multiplication then an addition and that in both sequences it amounts to a result of 2 + 3 or 3 + 2. Encourage pupils to compare the positions of other terms that appear in both sequences, for example 11 is the fourth term in Gianluca's and the third in Mathilde's, whereas 17 is seventh in Gianluca's and fifth in Mathilde's. Look for pupils who spot a difference of two place jumps in Mathilde's sequence and three place jumps in Gianluca's when the same number next appears in both.

In (c), check that pupils have used information they have reasoned from (b) to get the sequence 5, 11, 17, 23, 29. Check their methods of finding the sequence. Some pupils might recognise that by adding 1 to each matching term it changes to a sequence that is the 6 × table and as such can be adjusted to $t = 6n - 1$. A more fluent approach would be for pupils to look for the common difference and multiply this by n followed by an adjustment of −1 on every term.

Ask pupils to calculate the value when $n = 0$ in each of their sequences and ask them what this number reveals in the general term that they are seeking.

Challenge 3 Answer

a) 11 days

b) It is not possible. The number of members in the club at the end of any day will end in either 3 or 8 because it starts at 23 and 5 is added every day.

c) 17 days

Assessment

Have pupils set up a number sequence based on the information given in (a) and shown the sequence in table form so that they can reference the number of members each day and used information from the table to get to a general term?

days	n	0	1	2	3	4	5	...
members	t	23	28	33	38	43	48	...

Look for pupils who recognise that as the club already has 23 members, this can be seen as day '0'. Pupils should reason that from day zero, the position of each day (n) is multiplied by 5 followed by the addition of the initial 23 members. They should be able to reason from evidence that the number of members (t) can only end in a 3 or an 8.

Ask them if they know a times table that behaves in the same way (not ending in 3 or 8, but alternating between two different digits). You want them to say the 5 × table.

Ask them if they expect the number 78 to appear in the term row. Check that if they do expect to see 78 as a value of t they realise it is 30 more than the value on the 5th day. As five members are added each day, they should be able to work out 30 ÷ 5 = 6 more days so day 11 is when the club reaches 78 members.

In part (b), mathematical reasoning is required and not the ability to calculate. Pupils should reason that the number of members at the end of each day can only have 3 or 8 as the last digit and therefore 84 is not possible.

In (c), the question allows for the number 108 to appear in the t row. Pupils demonstrating a fluent approach and a high level of mastery will have organised the information into a general term $t = 5n + 23$ and will be able to substitute the value 108 for t and solve the equation by subtracting 23 from both sides and then dividing by 5.

Challenge 4 Answer

a) $t = 7n + 43$ or $t = 43 + 7n$ [43 + (number of weeks × 7)] when $t = $ £s in account and $n = $ number of weeks

b) 12 weeks

Assessment

Check that in (a) pupils organise the information in table form so that they are able to find a constant difference between each term. Look for pupils who decide that the figure £43 can be placed in the table at week 0.

weeks	n	0	1	2	3	4	5	...
£	t	43	50	57	64	71	78	...

Check that they are routinely checking for a common difference between each term (in this case 7) and that they are noting that in the first three cases this follows the rule $t = 7n + 43$.

Check that pupils are connecting the rule to the difference between each term plus the value of t at week 0.

Look for pupils who check this conjecture with $n = 4$ and $n = 5$ to see if it results in respective values of t.

In part (b), fluency is demonstrated if pupils can use the general term $t = 7n + 43$ and substitute the value t for 127 (127 = 7n + 43) and then subtract 43 from both sides (84 = 7n) and finally divide by 7 on both sides (12 = n), revealing the week number. This is perfectly acceptable in diagram format.

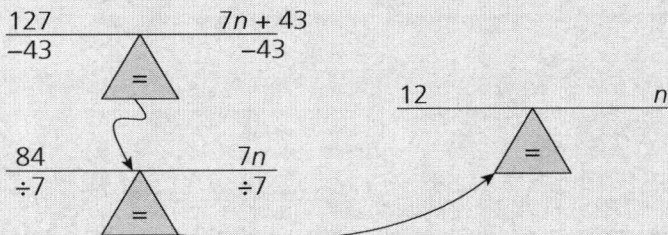

Algebra

How it all works

Challenge 5: Two packets of raisins and three packets of peanuts cost £1.20 altogether.

    a) If a packet of raisins costs 18p, how much would a packet of peanuts cost?

It is not possible to buy a 1p packet of raisins or peanuts in this shop.

    b) What could be the smallest cost for a packet of peanuts?

    c) What could be the smallest cost of a packet of raisins?

Challenge 6: Ali and Praia get £10 pocket money between them each week. If Ali received 80p extra he would get exactly the same amount as Praia.

    a) How much do they each get?

    b) For each of the next four weeks, Ali gets 25p more each week than the previous week and Praia gets 15p more. Who will receive the most pocket money at week 4?

    c) If they continued to receive this increased amount, is it possible that they would both receive the same pocket money and, if so, how many weeks would it take?

Challenge 7: A mind reader at a party told Stefan to do the following: 'Think of a number, multiply it by 2, add 4 to your answer, halve your result and subtract the number you first thought of.' She then told Stefan that his answer was 2. She was right because he was thinking of the number 5.

    a) Would it be a different answer if Stefan thought of 7 instead of 5?

    b) If Stefan's number = n, write an equation using all the mind reader's rules in the order she gave them to prove the result is always 2 for any number. (Hint: You might find adding brackets helpful.)

Challenge 8: Drawing pencils cost 23p and colouring pencils cost 35p.

    a) Is it possible to spend £1.74 and buy three drawing pencils? If so, how many colouring pencils would also have been bought?

    b) Start a number pattern where the rule is 'You must always have twice as many *colouring* pencils as *drawing* pencils'. Using this rule, how would you solve the cost of buying a mixture of 15 pencils altogether?

- *use simple formulae*
- *generate and describe linear number sequences*
- *express missing number problems algebraically*
- *find pairs of numbers that satisfy an equation with two unknowns*
- *enumerate possibilities of combinations of two variables*

Challenge 5 Answer

a) 28p **b)** 2p **c)** 3p

Assessment

Check that in (a), pupils realise that to calculate the cost of a packet of peanuts they must first subtract the cost of two packets of raisins from £1.20. This leaves £0.84, which is then divided by 3 to find the cost of one packet of peanuts.

Check in parts (b) and (c) that pupils can reason that although the cost of raisins can be an odd number, the cost of peanuts must be an even number because if it was an odd number, the cost of three packets would also be an odd number; when subtracted from £1.20 this would leave an odd number to be divided by 2, which is not possible. Armed with this knowledge, they can reason that the cheapest price for peanuts is 2p, the cheapest price for raisins is 3p as this leaves £1.14 to be divided by three packets of peanuts. Ask why raisins cannot cost 2p a packet. (It leaves a sum of £1.16 to be divided by 3, which is not a whole number result.)

Challenge 6 Answer

a) Ali gets £4.60 and Praia gets £5.40. **b)** Praia will get the most (£6.00).

c) It is possible and it would happen in week 8.

Assessment

In (a), pupils may solve the problem by using a diagram to calculate that Ali receives £4.60 and Praia £5.40 each week. Some pupils may use a more abstract approach.

Ali n / Praia n | 80p — £10   Ali n / Praia n — £9.20 n — $\dfrac{£9.20}{2}$ = £4.60

An efficient method for solving (b) is to multiply their increase by 4 then add this to their respective current allowances. Ali's sum is £4.60 + 4(25p) = £5.60. Even though Praia has a smaller increase, by week 4 she will have £5.40 + 4(15p) = £6.00.

In (c), they could calculate the answer by systematically adding the respective increases, but this would not show evidence of fluency at a high level. They might, however, construct a table (as below).

week	0	1	2	3	4	5	6	7	8
Ali	£4.60	£4.85	£5.10	£5.35	£5.60	£5.85	£6.10	£6.35	£6.60
Praia	£5.40	£5.55	£5.70	£5.85	£6.00	£6.15	£6.30	£6.45	£6.60

Ask pupils if they can find a general term for both sequences: Ali ($t = 25w + 460$), Praia ($t = 15w + 540$).

Challenge 7 Answer

a) No it would still be 2.

b) $\dfrac{2n + 4}{2} - n = 2$ or equivalent with brackets and division sign: $(2n + 4) \div 2 - n = 2$

Assessment

Check that in (a), pupils can fluently transfer the information in the challenge by substituting 7 for the missing number ($7 \times 2 = 14$, $14 + 4 = 18$, $18 \div 2 = 9$, $9 - 7 = 2$) to find that it is the same result for 7 as for 5.

Pupils might write (b) as a linear operation; if they haven't done so, they should be encouraged to simplify as they go through it.

$$n \longrightarrow n \times 2 \longrightarrow +4 \longrightarrow \div 2 \longrightarrow -n \qquad\qquad = 2$$

$$\quad (2n) \qquad (2n + 4) \qquad \dfrac{(2n + 4)}{2} \quad (n + 2 - n)$$

$$\downarrow$$

$$(n + 2)$$

The result is always 2 no matter which number you choose.

Ask pupils if they can construct a number sentence similar to the one in the challenge that will have the same answer every time. Observe how they decide on each stage of the information they give.

Challenge 8 Answer

a) Yes, you would have also bought three colouring pencils.

b) $d + 2d = 15$, $3d = 15$, $d = 5$ so 5 drawing, 10 colouring cost $5(23) + 10(35) = 465$; Cost = £4.65

Assessment

Check that in (a), pupils are multiplying 23p by 3 (69p) and then subtracting from £1.74 leaving £1.05, which they should then divide by 35p to find out how many colouring pencils were bought. Check that pupils are using the same units for ease of calculation (converting the sums to pence). Check that they attempt to calculate an answer mentally.

In (b), check that pupils recognise that they are creating numbers from a strict rule, but that it does not have to be a complicated rule. Have pupils considered that the rule is saying that for every one drawing pencil you must have two colouring pencils? Do pupils see the problem as a number of sets of three pencils with 15 pencils in total?

Check that pupils multiply the general group of pencils (3) by 5 to get to the 15 pencils altogether. Encourage pupils to then multiply 1 drawing pencil by 5 (5 altogether) followed by 2 colouring pencils by 5 (10 altogether and with the drawing pencils 15 altogether).

Check that they then multiply 23p and 35p by 5 and 10 respectively to get the cost of both sets of pencils (drawing = £1.15 and colouring = £3.50) and that they add these to get the total (£4.65).

Ask pupils if it would be possible to buy 25 pencils altogether if you must have three colouring pencils for every drawing pencil. Look for them to reason that as 25 is not a multiple of 4 it is not possible.

Measurement

Time and distance

Challenge 1: The coach from Penzance to Chichester leaves one morning at quarter past seven. The same bus gets back to Penzance and starts the journey again exactly 437 minutes later.

a) What time does it leave for its second journey? Give your answer in 24-hour time.

b) On this second journey, the bus has a puncture which makes it 53 minutes late for the next trip from Penzance. What time does it leave Penzance on its third trip?

c) Chichester to Penzance is approximately 405km. Convert this to miles (to the nearest mile).

Challenge 2: The people of Timetown use decimal notation to read and tell the time. The following times are given in decimal notation. What exact time do you think they represent? Write your answers using 12-hour clock time.

a) 10.4   **b)** 19.333…   **c)** 0.75

d) What time would 2.36pm read in Timetown?

Challenge 3: In the long jump on sports day, Jamie jumped 1.86m and Trevor managed 23cm more.

a) What was Trevor's recorded jump in metres?

b) Including Jagjit's jump, the total of the three jumps was 5.93m. Was Jagjit's jump closer to Jamie's or Trevor's?

Challenge 4: Square wall tiles are arranged as shown to give a shape with a perimeter of 112.8cm.

a) Donna thinks this arrangement produces the greatest perimeter length possible. Is she right? Explain your reasoning.

b) Donna also thinks it is possible to arrange them in other ways and still have a perimeter of 112.8cm. How many ways can you find? Can you explain a rule that you used to help you find the different shapes?

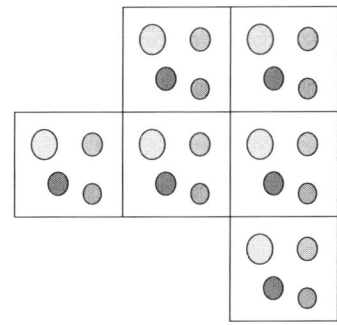

- **solve problems involving the calculation and conversion of units of measure, using decimal notation up to three decimal places where appropriate**
- **use, read, write and convert between standard units, converting measurements of length, mass, volume and time from a smaller unit of measure to a larger unit, and vice versa, using decimal notation to up to three decimal places**
- **convert between miles and kilometres**
- **recognise that shapes with the same areas can have different perimeters and vice versa**

Challenge 1 Answer

a) 1432

b) 2242

c) 253 miles

Assessment

Check that in (a), pupils are using the same unit of measurement for all times. It is probably useful to encourage the use of 24-hour time as that is what the answer asks for.

Check that they convert the starting time to 0715.

Check that they are using a well-chosen division method to convert the time taken for the journey (437 minutes) into hours and minutes. Are they using this opportunity to solve with long division?

$$
\begin{array}{r}
7\ \text{r}\ 17 \\
60\,\overline{)4\ 3\ 7} \\
4\ 2\ 0 \\
\hline
1\ 7
\end{array}
$$

Get pupils to confirm that the remainder 17 is 17 minutes as it was minutes that were being divided to produce an hours and minutes alternative. Check that when they add the 24-hour times 0715 and 0717 they realise that there are two different number bases to be aware of (in 0717, the 07 is base 10 but the 17 is base 60).

A similar process will get a successful conclusion in part (b). Check that pupils reason that a normal measurement of time for the journey is 437 minutes or 7 hours 17 minutes. Check that they are routinely adding the stoppage time to this (53 minutes) to get either 490 minutes or 8 hours 10 minutes initially.

Check that they convert this to 24-hour time for efficiency of calculation (0810) and then add this to the time the coach left Penzance (1432), giving a third departure time of 2242 (1432 + 0810).

It would be prudent to supplement this challenge with one or two exercises to allow pupils to practise adding times. For example: 'Add the two 24-hour times 1145 and 0737.' and 'The current time is 1051. What time will it be in three and a half hours? Give your answer in 24-hour clock time.'

In (c), check that pupils know that 1 kilometre $\approx \frac{5}{8}$ mile. They should use this knowledge to multiply 405 by $\frac{5}{8}$ (253.125 miles) and round to 253 miles.

Challenge 2 Answer

a)   10.4 = 10:24am   **b)**   19.333… = 7:20pm   **c)**   0.75 = 12:45am   **d)**   2:36pm = 14.6

Assessment

Check that in (a), pupils understand that in 10.4, 10 represents hours and 0.4 represents $\frac{4}{10}$ of an hour. They should reason that as $\frac{1}{10}$ of an hour is six minutes, $\frac{4}{10}$ is 24 minutes and therefore the time in 12-hour clock time is 10:24am.

In (b), fluency of operation will be demonstrated if pupils can convert 0.333… to the fraction $\frac{1}{3}$ and convert this to 20 minutes. They should also realise that they need to subtract 12 from 19 to get the 12-hour version of the time (7:20pm).

In (c), pupils should recognise that 0 in 0.75 represents midnight and convert the time accordingly to 12:45am.

Part (d) requires different thinking. Check that pupils convert the minutes to a fraction out of 60 $(\frac{36}{60})$ and simplify this to $\frac{6}{10}$ and then convert to the equivalent decimal (0.6), which they should add to the hour part. The hour part indicates that the time is past noon so they will need to add 12, arriving at the final result of 14.6.

Challenge 3 Answer

a)   2.09m

b)   Jagjit jumped 1.98m, therefore his jump was closer to Trevor's.

Assessment

Check that in (a), pupils are first making all units of measurement the same before completing the addition to find Trevor's jump (1.86m + 0.23m = 2.09m).

In part (b), pupils need to find the sum of Trevor's and Jamie's jumps first, then subtract this from 5.93m to find the measurement of Jagjit's jump. Look for pupils demonstrating this reasoning and using a structured procedure or using an efficient mental calculation strategy. Are they using formal addition and subtraction and routinely checking answers with inverse procedures?

$$
\begin{array}{r}
1.86 \\
+\ 2.09 \\
\hline
3.95 \\
1
\end{array}
\qquad
\begin{array}{r}
^{4\ 18}5.\overset{1}{9}3 \\
-\ 3.95 \\
\hline
1.98 \\
\end{array}
\qquad
\begin{array}{r}
1.98 \\
+\ 3.95 \\
\hline
5.93 \\
1\ 1
\end{array}
$$

When pupils have calculated Jagjit's jump, check their reasoning about which of the other two jumps his is closest to. This is an ideal opportunity to assess mathematical reasoning. Question pupils about how they decided on their answer.

Show the diagram below and ask if they agree with its reasoning. They may argue that it is not necessary to do this for this problem, but check that they understand that by using this method, the differences between the measurements are not altered and an easier calculation is enabled.

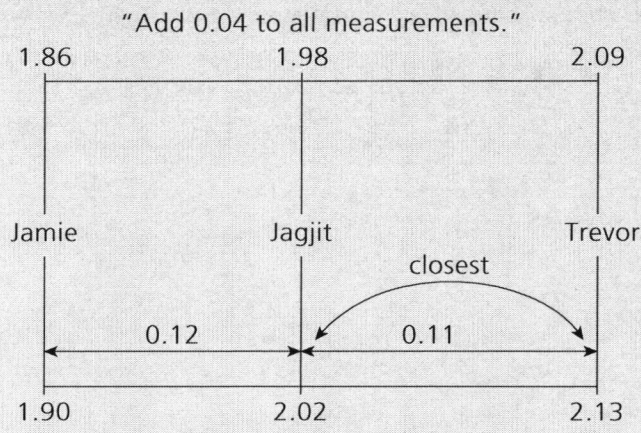

Challenge 4 Answer

a) Donna is incorrect. If the tiles are lined up in a 6 × 1 array the perimeter will be 14 times the length of a tile.

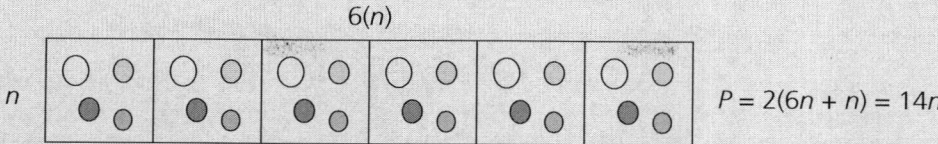

$$P = 2(6n + n) = 14n$$

b) 6 ways:

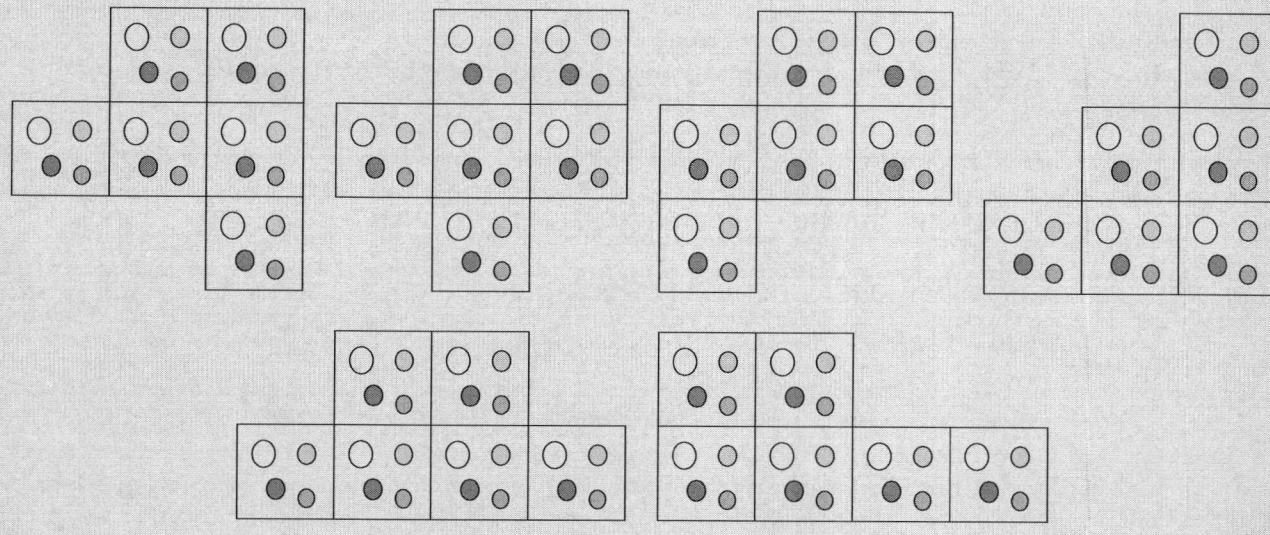

Assessment

Check for mathematical reasoning in (a) rather than a pure process of calculation. Check that pupils know that the maximum perimeter for any shape is made when each square used exposes the maximum number of edges. In the diagram below, the numbers represent the edges included in the perimeter.

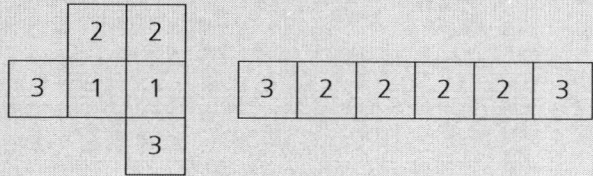

Using this reasoning should make it clear that the 6 × 1 array has a greater perimeter; further examination will conclude that this arrangement has the greatest possible perimeter of any shape made from this number of tiles and it avoids any use of the given decimal length of the perimeter of the shape (112.8cm).

In (b), if pupils have used the reasoning that the perimeter of the given shape consists of 2 + 2 + 3 + 1 + 1 + 3 = 12 edges then they can avoid calculating the length of one edge. They can also play with the number of edges available to them. There are six squares and a total of 12 edges so they could find different combinations of the numbers 1, 2 and 3 that can be exposed in the shapes (4 cannot be used as that would mean a square by itself and they must all meet another square on one edge). They could also work out how many ways this can be done even though they are not asked to find the maximum number of shapes available. Although not a mathematical rule in a well-defined sense, this shows a very high level of reasoning.

Measurement

Perimeters

Challenge 5: A rectangle measures 8cm by 3cm.

    a) Draw and label a right-angled triangle with half the area of the rectangle.

    b) Draw and label an isosceles triangle with half the area of the rectangle.

    c) Draw and label three different triangles with areas equal to the rectangle.

Challenge 6: A gardener has 900m² of turf to lay and needs to put a wooden fence around its perimeter. Fencing comes in 10m sections that cost £32 a section.

    a) What is the minimum he must spend on fencing to complete this job?

    b) An 800m² field also has to be turfed. He says the fencing for this job should cost less than the first job. Do you agree?

Challenge 7: A maths teacher says there is not enough information on the diagram of the rectilinear shape to be able to calculate its perimeter. Do you agree? If there is enough information, then calculate the perimeter.

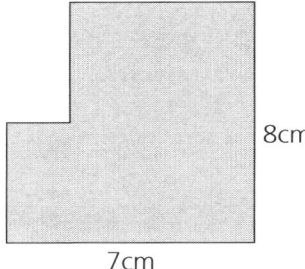

8cm

7cm

Challenge 8: Jenny says that the perimeter of this rectilinear shape is exactly 68cm. Do you agree or disagree? What is your reasoning?

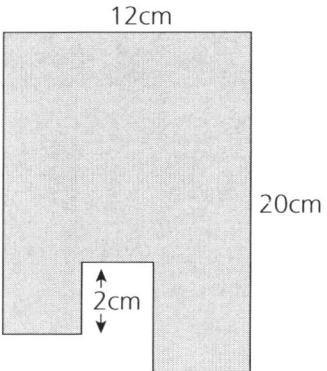

12cm

20cm

2cm

National Curriculum objectives, Year 6, Measurement

- *solve problems involving the calculation and conversion of units of measure, using decimal notation up to three decimal places where appropriate*
- *recognise that shapes with the same areas can have different perimeters and vice versa*
- *recognise when it is possible to use formula for area and volume of shapes*
- *calculate the area of parallelograms and triangles*

Challenge 5 Answer

a) For example:

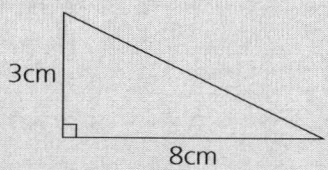

b) For example:

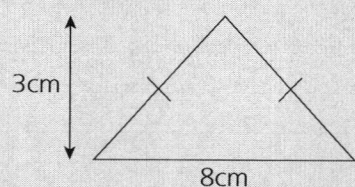

c) Any three different triangles each with base and height that are a pair of factors of 48, for example:

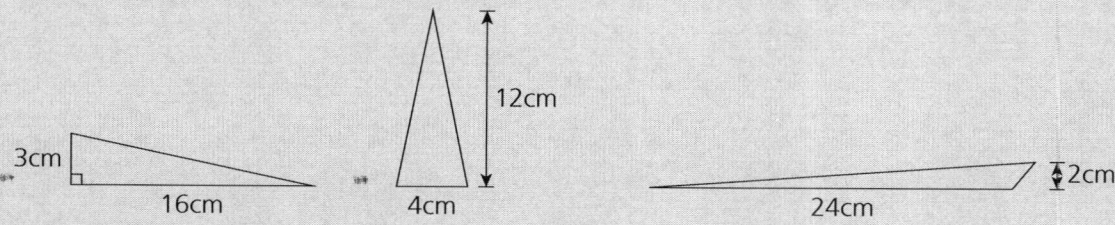

Assessment

In (a), check that pupils recognise that a diagonal drawn between opposite corners in any rectangle cuts the shape into two halves, both of which are right-angled triangles, and that each, by definition, has half the area of the rectangle.

In (b), pupils have the opportunity to go for a direct answer by taking a central point on the base or height and drawing lines to the two opposite corners (see diagram).

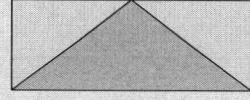
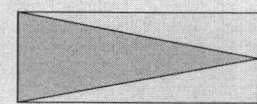

This is not the only solution. More inquisitive pupils may use the fact that the area of the isosceles triangle is half that of the rectangle ($24cm^2 \div 2 = 12cm^2$) and use this to construct other rectangles with an area of $24cm^2$ and then follow the process above.

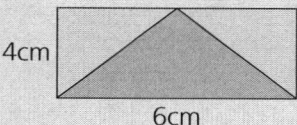
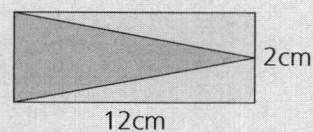

In (c), pupils should reason that in order to draw triangles equal in area to an 8 × 3 rectangle they need a reference rectangle twice the area of this (48cm²), which can be constructed by using factor pairs of 48. In order to complete this task, they need only find three factor pairs as in the examples below.

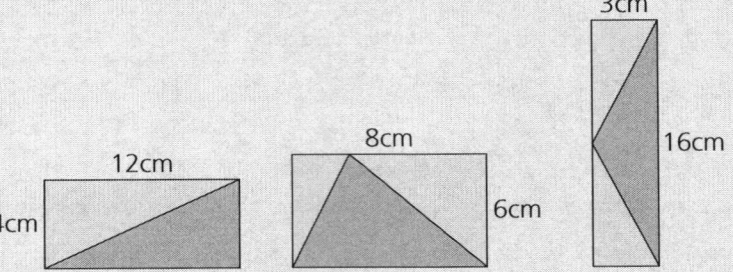

Challenge 6 Answer

a) £384

b) Disagree, the minimum he can spend is £384.

Assessment

Check that pupils recognise that they need to find factor pairs of 900 that are each multiples of 10 in order for the fencing to fit. Observe how systematic pupils are when they search for factors of 900. For example, did they find the factors and then pair them off from the smallest onwards?

{1, ..., 900}

{1, 2, ..., 450, 900}

{1, 2, 3, 4, 5, 6, 7, 8, 9, 10, 12, 15, 18, 20, 25, **30**, 36, 45, 50, 60, 75, 90, 100, 150, 180, 225, 300, 450, 900}

Check that pupils are convinced that there are only two possibilities for the dimensions of the field to be turfed in order that the fencing supplied will fit (10m × 90m and 30m × 30m). Check that they reason that a 30m × 30m field will cost less to fence as the perimeter is the smaller of the two (120m). They should be able to then divide the perimeter by 10 to find that 12 panels will be sufficient and then complete a simple multiplication of £32 by 12 to get the cost (£384).

A similar approach for part (b) should be considered by pupils where they first look for factor pairs of 800 that are both multiples of 10 (20 × 40 and 10 × 80). If they follow the same reasoning as in (a) they will see that the 20m × 40m area will also cost £32 × 12 = £384 while the 10m × 80m area will cost £32 × 18 = £576. This will prove that the gardener is wrong and that it will cost at the very least the same as the first field.

Challenge 7 Answer

There is enough information; the perimeter is 30cm.

Assessment

Ask pupils what is meant by rectilinear shape. They should understand that this type of figure is a polygon with an even number of sides that either meet at 90° or 270°; if this is not firmly understood, the problem cannot be attempted.

Check to see if pupils can convince themselves, each other or you that the diagram has two sets of two lines that can be added to give the same length as one of the labelled sides.

In the diagram, pupils should be clear that $a + b$ = 7cm and $c + d$ = 8cm. By stating this they should be able to affirm that the perimeter is 2 × 7cm + 2 × 8cm = 30cm.

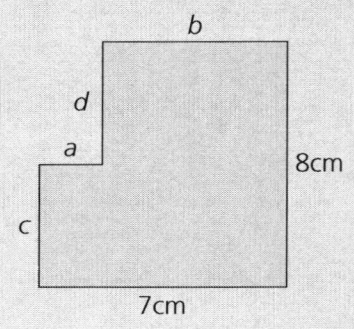

Some pupils may be able to explain that because the lines all meet at right angles, line *a* can be 'moved' vertically next to line *b* and line *d* can be moved horizontally next to *c*, which would form a 7cm × 8cm rectangle.

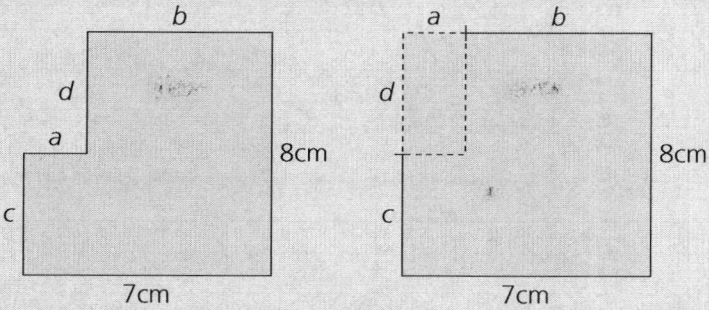

Challenge 8 Answer

Agree, the perimeter is 68cm.

Assessment

Ask pupils if they agree that this is a rectilinear shape and ask them to explain what makes it rectilinear. Ask if they think it is a good idea to label the unknown sides with letters to help them make statements about the sums of two sides that are possibly the same as one longer side.

Check that a diagram has been created similar to the one below.

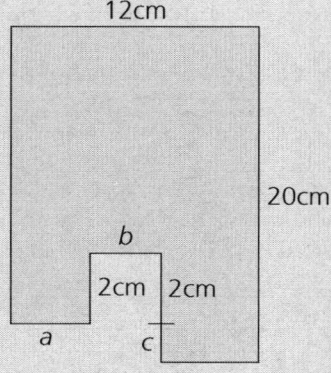

Have they reasoned that the line labelled 2cm + c is possible because of the parallel length of 2cm opposite it?

Check that as in the previous challenge they are able to make sense of the rectilinear nature of the figure by moving sides horizontally and vertically. Check that they acknowledge that the rectangle formed has two extra 2cm lengths and that the sum of these extra lengths must be added when calculating the perimeter: 2(12cm + 20cm) + 2(2cm) = 68cm.

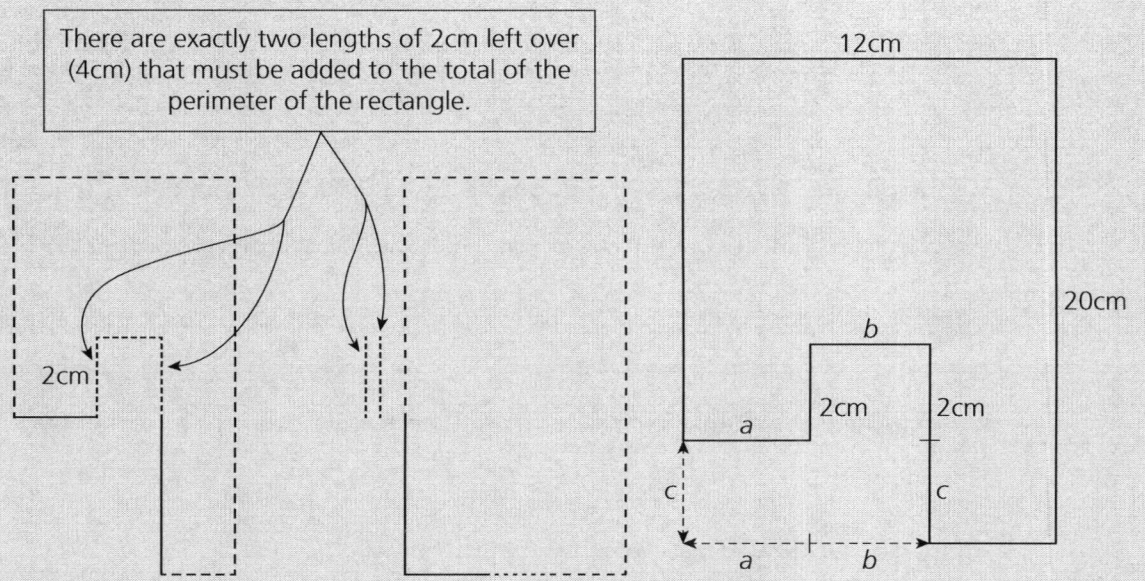

There are exactly two lengths of 2cm left over (4cm) that must be added to the total of the perimeter of the rectangle.

Measurement

Measuring shapes

Challenge 9:   A football has a diameter of 20cm.

    a)   One of these footballs is packaged in a square-faced cardboard box. The ball touches the box on every one of its sides. What is the surface area of the box?

    b)   How much cardboard would be needed to make a box that contained three of these footballs sat on top of each other?

    c)   Is it true that the volume of the second box is three times that of the first?

Challenge 10:   Gemma says that she can work out the exact area of a square whose vertices all touch the circumference of a circle with a diameter of 40cm. Does she have enough information to do this? If so, what is the area of the square?

Challenge 11:   A rectangular piece of canvas 65cm × 30cm has to be cut into five triangles to make sails for a model boat.

    a)   David says two of the triangles must be right-angled triangles. Do you think he is right? Explain your reasoning.

    b)   Two of the triangles have respective areas of 300cm^2 and 600cm^2. What could the base lengths of the other three triangles be?

Challenge 12:   Four identical paper parallelograms have been joined end-to-end to form a circular strip. The area of the circular strip is 100cm^2.

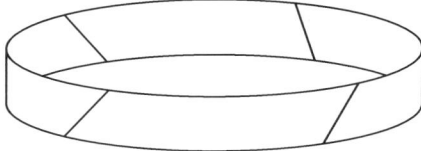

    a)   Is it possible to make the same ring with four identical rectangles instead of parallelograms? If it is, what would be true about each parallelogram and rectangle?

    b)   Draw and label a parallelogram and a rectangle so that four are needed to make circular strips with an area of 240cm². You can choose the dimensions of the rectangle and parallelogram, but the circular strips they make must have an area of 240cm².

    c)   Is it possible to make a circular strip with an area of 240cm² using four identical rectangles or parallelograms with a width of 14cm?

National Curriculum objectives, Year 6, Measurement

- solve problems involving the calculation and conversion of units of measure, using decimal notation up to three decimal places where appropriate
- use, read, write and convert between standard units, converting measurements of length, mass, volume and time from a smaller unit of measure to a larger unit, and vice versa, using decimal notation to up to three decimal places
- recognise that shapes with the same areas can have different perimeters and vice versa
- recognise when it is possible to use formula for area and volume of shapes
- calculate the area of parallelograms and triangles
- calculate, estimate and compare volume of cubes and cuboids using standard units, including cubic centimetres (cm³) and cubic metres (m³), and extending to other units [for example, mm³ and km³]

Challenge 9 Answer

a)   2400cm²

b)   5600cm²

c)   Yes, box 1 has a volume of 8000cm³ and box 2 has a volume of 24 000cm³.

Assessment

Check that pupils have identified that the profile of a football is circular and encompassed this within a square to determine the area of one face of the box.

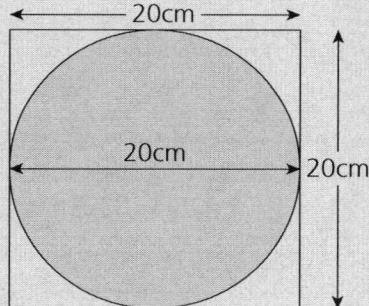

Check that they know that a net of six of these squares is needed to make the box in (a) and that they can calculate the total surface area (6 × 20cm × 20cm = 2400cm²). Check that they do not actually draw the net as it is not needed to solve this part of the problem.

In part (b), they might find it useful to draw a diagram of the net and to calculate the surface area of each panel that makes it up. Check that they understand that the packaging will now be a cuboid with a length of three diameters of the ball (60cm) and that there will be four of these faces, plus another two of 20cm × 20cm, one at each end.

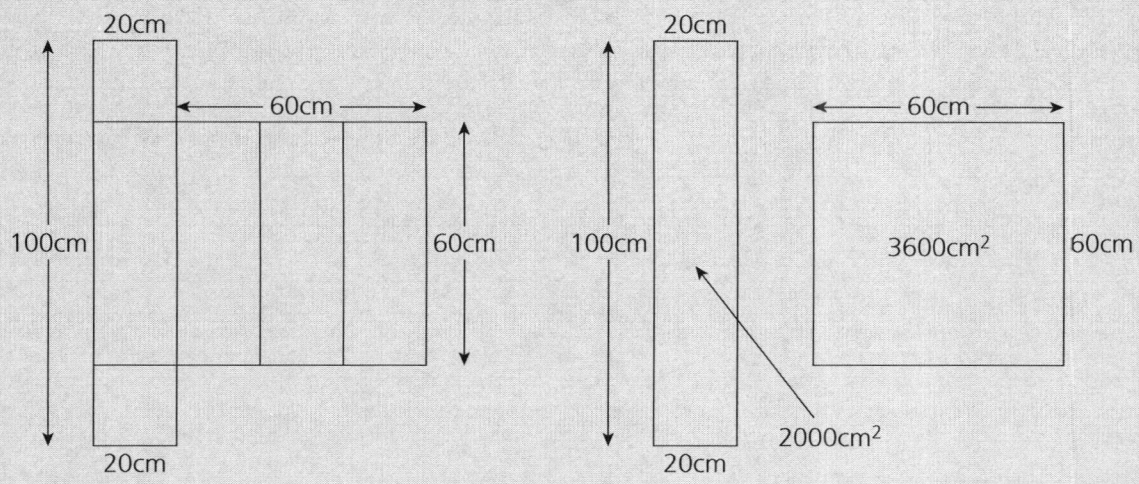

Fluency at this stage will be demonstrated by their ability to calculate the area of the net by dividing it into two (or more) rectangles and so find the surface area of the box (5600cm²).

In (c), encourage pupils to use intuition based on one box holding one ball and the other box holding three balls to guide their thinking before they calculate the actual volumes of each box. Allow them to sketch the boxes and label them before calculation takes place if this helps.

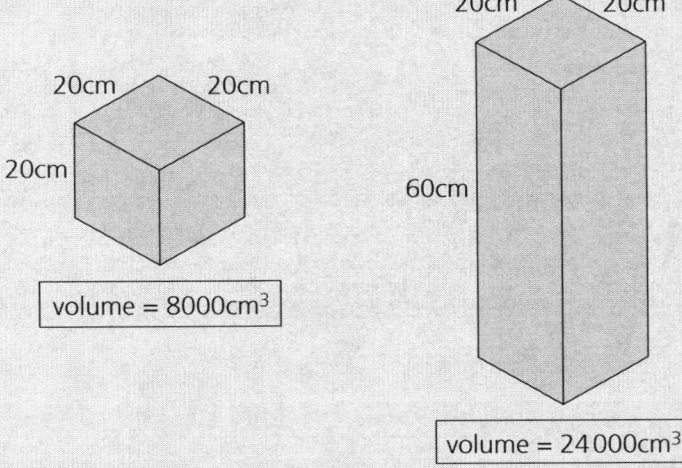

Check that they use knowledge of the 8× table and not lengthy written methods to confirm that the volume of the larger box will be three times the volume of the smaller.

Challenge 10 Answer

Gemma is correct, she has enough information to work out that the area of the square is 800cm².

Assessment

Pupils will need to use their understanding of the area of right-angled triangles to complete this challenge.

Check that they draw two diagonal lines joining the vertices so that the square is divided into four equal right-angled triangles.

Can they reason that each of the right-angled triangles they have created has identical sides that meet at the right angle and that these sides all measure 20cm? Ask them to explain why they measure 20cm. (Each side is exactly half the diameter of the circle.)

Check that pupils can calculate the area of each triangle by multiplying the base (20cm) by the height (20cm) and dividing by 2 to get an area of 200cm². Ask them to remind you why this formula works when looking for the area of a triangle (two right-angled triangles can be arranged to form a rectangle with the same base and height).

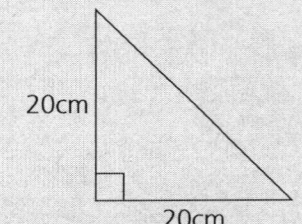

Check that they multiply this area by four to get a total area of 800cm² for the enclosed square.

Ask pupils to make a labelled drawing of the square in the circle divided into four right-angled triangles and another of a square made from two of the same right-angled triangles. Ask pupils to visually compare them and ask if they think one looks to have twice the area of the other. Get them to draw them side by side and compare them. Ask them to confirm mathematically how many times bigger the larger square is than the smaller one to see if they use the reasoning that they must be twice as big because there are four of the smaller triangles in the large square and two in the smaller one. They might not say this because visually it is not so convincing. However, this would be an opportunity to assess mathematical reasoning.

Challenge 11 Answer

a) David is not right. He is correct that two right-angled triangles can be created by utilising the height of the rectangle, **but** it is also possible to have five triangular sails that do not contain any right angles.

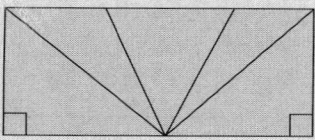 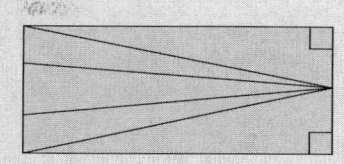 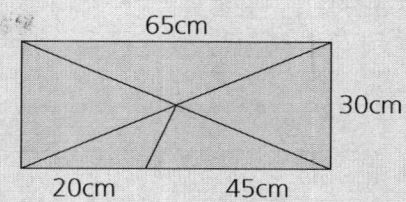

b) There are many possible answers. For example, as the areas of the triangles are given, the height of the rectangle can be used (30cm), leaving the base to join each height at 20cm and 40cm to form triangles with the required areas. If completed like this, an extra triangle can also be placed on the remaining base length (5cm) whose area can also be found. Finally, the apex of this triangle splits the other base length into two lengths (*a* cm and *b* cm) of the pupils' choice.

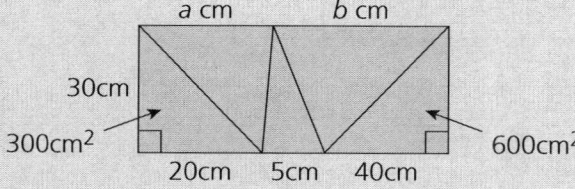

Assessment

Pupils will need to experiment to complete (a). Ask them if they think it is possible to cut two right-angled triangles from the canvas and what the remaining shape might be. They should be able to say that it is possible to have two right-angled triangles and that the remaining shape would be a four-sided polygon. Their reasoning might be tested further by asking if it is possible that a polygon with more than four sides could be left. Try to draw out of them that only a four-sided shape can be left, which must be a trapezium, which in turn could be made of three triangles.

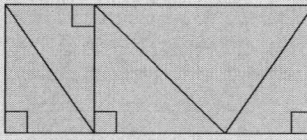
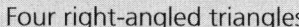

Four-sided polygons – more specifically, both are trapeziums

Press pupils further by asking them if it is possible to have more than two right-angled triangles and then ask them if they think it is possible for only one of the triangles or none of them to be right angled.

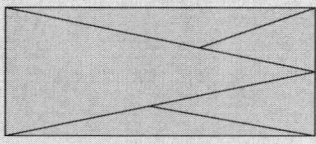

Four right-angled triangles   No right-angled triangles

Pupils might suggest that if five triangles are to be cut then there must be an even number of right-angled triangles. If they do, you might ask them to investigate whether the same is true if six triangles had to be cut. Investigation should result in the conclusion that a single right-angled triangle is possible when cutting five triangles.

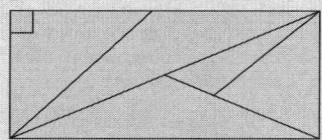

Pupils might find (b) more accessible if they assume the triangles with the given areas of 300cm² and 600cm² are two right-angled triangles at either end of the rectangle and use the height of 30cm to calculate the given areas of the triangles. Check that they firstly draw two rectangles within the canvas with areas of 600cm² and 1200cm² and then draw diagonals to form the right-angled triangles using knowledge of how to calculate the area of triangles to calculate the length of the base of each triangle (20cm and 40cm).

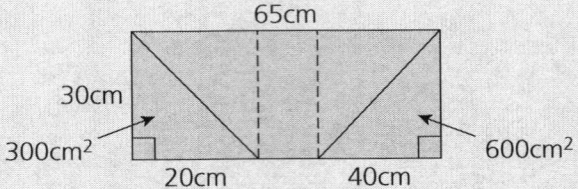

Pupils now need to calculate the base lengths of the other three triangles. Check that they are confident that the base length of one of them must be 5cm (65cm – 20cm – 40cm if the right-angled triangles shown in the diagram above are used) and that a point can be placed somewhere along the top of the rectangle to separate the length into two lengths (*a* and *b*) such that *a* + *b* = 65cm.

Ask pupils if this is the only way the problem can be solved. Ask if it is possible to draw two different triangles that have areas of 300cm² and 600cm² (see diagram below).

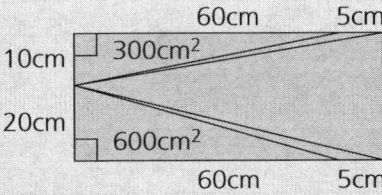

Challenge 12 Answer

a) It is possible. The lengths and perpendicular widths of both the parallelogram and the rectangle are identical.

b) One rectangle and one parallelogram with bh = 60. For example:

c) This is only possible if fractional lengths are permitted. Each strip must have an area of 60cm². A division of the area (60cm²) by 14 results in $4\frac{2}{7}$.

Assessment

In (a), pupils should be able to reason that for this to be correct, each rectangle and each parallelogram would need to have an area of 25cm² as this is the area of the strip divided by 4. Examples of how this can be achieved are shown below.

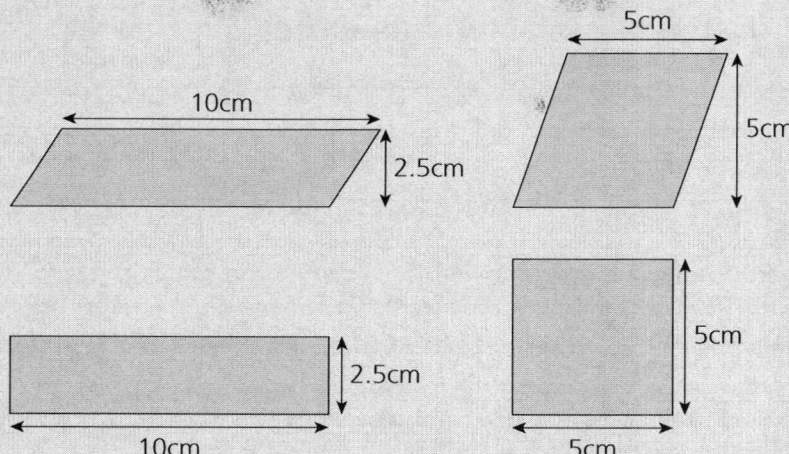

They should be able to state that the heights and bases of respective pairs of parallelograms and rectangles are equal. You might consider asking pupils who arrive at this conclusion if they can prove that the area of the parallelogram is identical to that of its paired rectangle.

When they come to (b), pupils should use information from (a) to reason that each rectangle and parallelogram should have an area of 240 ÷ 4cm² (60cm²) and use pairs of factors of 60 to construct the shapes. For example:

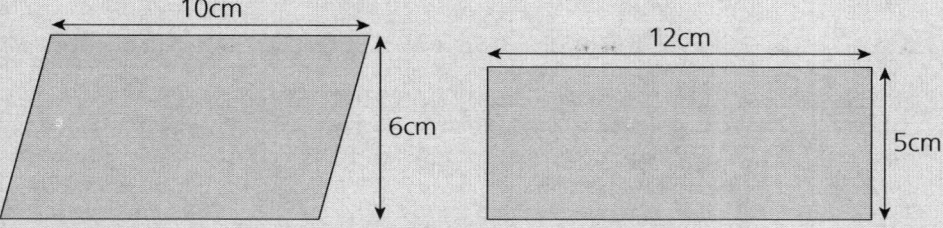

More creative mathematicians might look for non-whole number solutions to show that the result is not restricted to whole numbers (8cm × 7.5cm strips would satisfy the problem).

In part (c), check that pupils are aware that if 14cm was the base of a rectangle or parallelogram, the height would be the value that gave a product of 60 when multiplied by 14. Check they use formal division methods to solve this and round to an appropriate number of decimal places.

Estimate 60 ÷ 14 ≈ 4

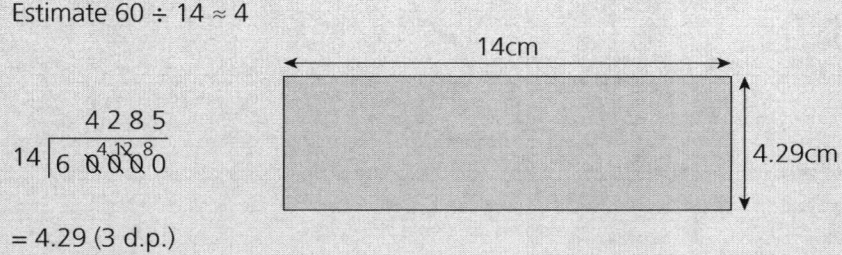

= 4.29 (3 d.p.)

This reasoning and calculation should enable pupils to answer the question.

Measurement

Different dimensions

Challenge 13: Jo has a tray of 2cm × 2cm × 2cm cubes. She wants to make larger cubes with them and record how many of the small cubes it takes.

    a) Can she make a larger cube using eight of the smaller cubes? Explain your reason.

    b) How many cubes would it take to make a cube with a base length of three cubes?

    c) Jo wants to make a cube with a base length of four cubes. How many cubes will she need?

    d) She says that she can make only one cuboid with eight cubes. Do you agree?

    e) What is the volume of a 2cm × 2cm × 2cm cube in mm³?

Challenge 14: A square and a rectangle both have areas of 36m².

    a) Draw a square and some rectangles with areas of 36m² that have dimensions that are whole centimetres. How many can you draw?

    b) Which shape has the smallest perimeter?

    c) Which shape has the largest perimeter?

    d) What can be said about perimeters and areas of squares and rectangles?

Challenge 15: A square is a special type of rectangle. The formula for finding the perimeter of a rectangle is $2(b + h)$ where b is the base length and h is the vertical height of the rectangle.

    a) If the perimeter of a rectangle is 30cm, the shape cannot be a square with a whole number side length, but it could be at least three different rectangles with whole number side lengths.

        Do you agree with this statement? How many rectangles with whole number lengths are there?

b) How many rectangles with whole number side lengths could be made from a perimeter of:

i) 4cm? **ii)** 16cm? **iii)** 64cm?

c) You are told that the perimeter of a rectangle is an even square number and the lengths of all the sides are a whole number. Think of a rule that would allow you to work out how many different rectangles you could make. Test your conjecture on a rectangle with a perimeter of 144.

Challenge 16: From what you know about the relationship between perimeters and areas of rectangles, what do you predict can be said about the surface areas of cubes and cuboids with identical volumes?

For example, investigate this diagram of a cube and two cuboids with identical volumes. What is happening as the cuboid gets longer for example?

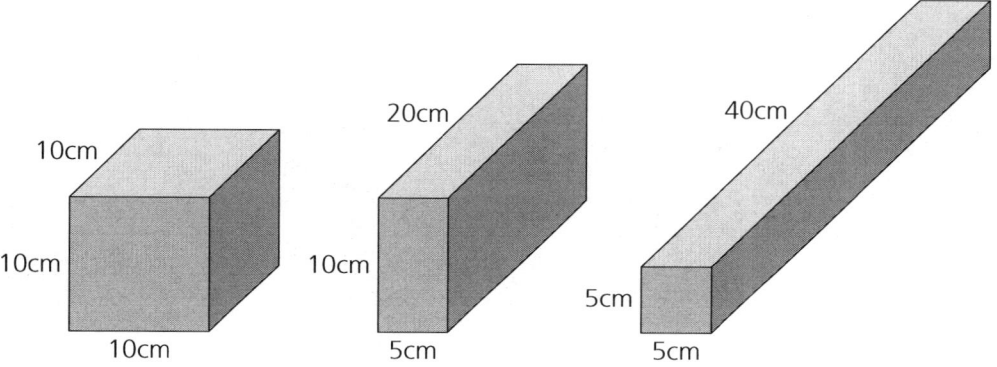

Challenge 13 Answer

a)   Yes, it is possible. The larger cube will have a width of 2 cubes, depth 2 cubes, height 2 cubes: $2 \times 2 \times 2 =$ 8 cubes.

b)   27 cubes ($3 \times 3 \times 3$)

c)   64 cubes ($4 \times 4 \times 4$)

d)   No, there are three possibilities in total:

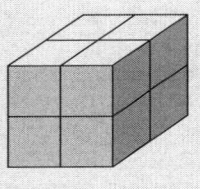

e)   8000mm³

Assessment

In (a), pupils might recognise 8 as a cube number ($2 \times 2 \times 2 = 8$) and realise that it is possible to make a bigger cube from that number of smaller cubes. If they don't, then use concrete equipment linked to the relationship to 2 (width) × 2 (length) × 2 (height) = 8.

In (b), pupils are expected to use the reasoning from (a) to arrive at the conclusion that 27 cubes will be needed ($3 \times 3 \times 3$). By the time they reach (c), pupils should be fluently stating that the result (64 cubes) is found by multiplying $4 \times 4 \times 4$.

When pupils start on (d), there are useful links that they should be making. The first one is that a cube is a specific type of cuboid so a $2 \times 2 \times 2$ cube is one cuboid that can be made with eight cubes. The second link they need to make is to how factors can help lead to the solution for every cuboid with whole number dimensions. Pupils who can string three numbers in a multiplication that has a product of 8 will be displaying high levels of fluency based on mathematical reasoning. This reasoning will allow them to state there are two more cuboids besides the $2 \times 2 \times 2$ cube: $1 \times 1 \times 8$ and $1 \times 2 \times 4$ are also possible. They should be able to back this up with equipment if asked.

In (e), they might find it useful to draw a cube and label it using the 2cm measurement converted to millimetres to be clear about the multiplication of the dimensions.

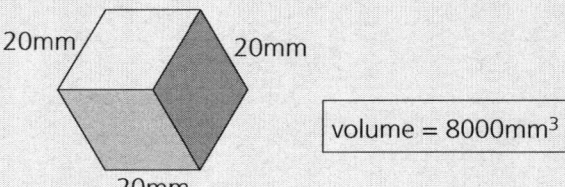

volume = 8000mm³

Challenge 14 Answer

a)

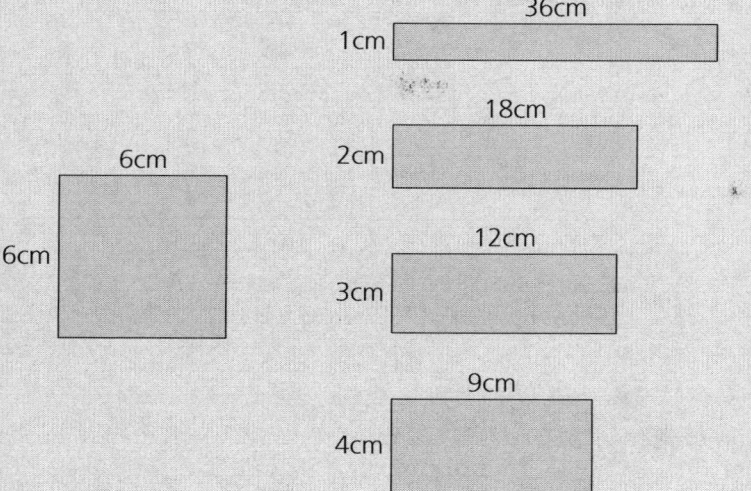

b) The square has the smallest perimeter.

c) The 1cm × 36cm rectangle has the largest perimeter.

d) When a square and a number of rectangles are equal in area, the square will always have the smallest perimeter and the rectangle with the longest individual side will have the largest perimeter. When a square and number of rectangles all have identical perimeters, as the rectangle gets closer to the 'look' of a square the area gets larger. The more square looking the shape, the shorter the perimeter and larger the area; the more elongated the rectangle, the longer the perimeter and smaller the area.

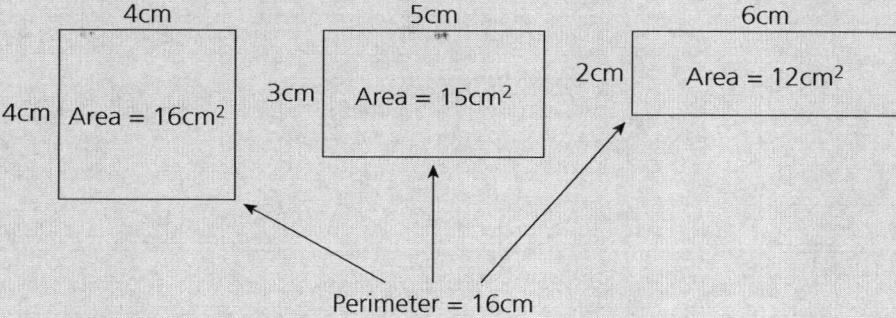

Assessment

Pupils should be able to link (a) to the factors of 36. If they know the factors of 36 (1, 2, 3, 4, 6, 9, 12, 18 and 36), they will be able to state with confidence that five rectangles including a square can be drawn. Check that they use a systematic approach to make sure no factor pairs are overlooked. For example:

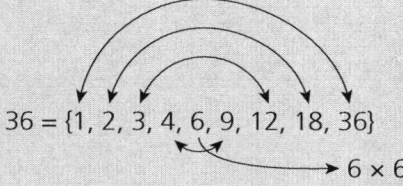

In (b), pupils showing reasonable fluency should add the height and base of each rectangle then multiply by 2 to calculate each perimeter. They will state that the square has the shortest perimeter.

In (c), check that they can explain that the longest and narrowest rectangle is the one with the largest perimeter.

In (d), pupils should be encouraged to state that as a rectangle gets closer in shape to a square its perimeter gets smaller and that as a rectangle gets longer and narrower its perimeter becomes larger.

Challenge 15 Answer

a) Pupils should agree with the statement and show three of the seven possible rectangles.

b) **i)** 1   **ii)** 4   **iii)** 16

c) If the perimeter is an even square number and it is divided by 4, the result is how many different rectangles can be made with whole number side lengths. A perimeter of 144 divided by 4 is 36, which is the number of rectangles that can be made.

Assessment

Pupils might attempt (a) by first halving 30 (= 15) and then systematically finding each pair of whole number addition solutions to 15. If they created a systematic table, for example, they would be able to establish that the statement is correct and also state that there are seven rectangles with a perimeter of 30cm.

Sum to 15	
1 +	14
2 +	13
3 +	12
4 +	11
5 +	10
6 +	9
7 +	8

Pupils could be challenged to make a conjecture about the type of number that would always allow a square to be made. (An even number as they can be halved, which allows height and base to be equal. It can never work with an odd number total of base and height.)

Pupils who had success in (a) should be fluently halving each of the numbers in (b) then finding all the whole number pairs that make its total.

Part (c) is an investigation. Check that pupils are not randomly choosing different side lengths of available squares, but that they start with the smaller ones and look for a pattern (linking the subject matter to algebra also).

Square	Perimeter	Rectangles with this perimeter
2 × 2	8	2
4 × 4	16	4
6 × 6	24	6
8 × 8	32	8

Again, a table would be a systematic way to gather information that would suggest that if the perimeter is divided by 4 the result is how many rectangles with whole number sides can be constructed. Pupils may also see the more obvious link to the sides of the square from which they started.

Challenge 16 Answer

As the cuboid becomes more cube like, the surface area becomes smaller or as a cuboid becomes less cube like, the surface area becomes larger.

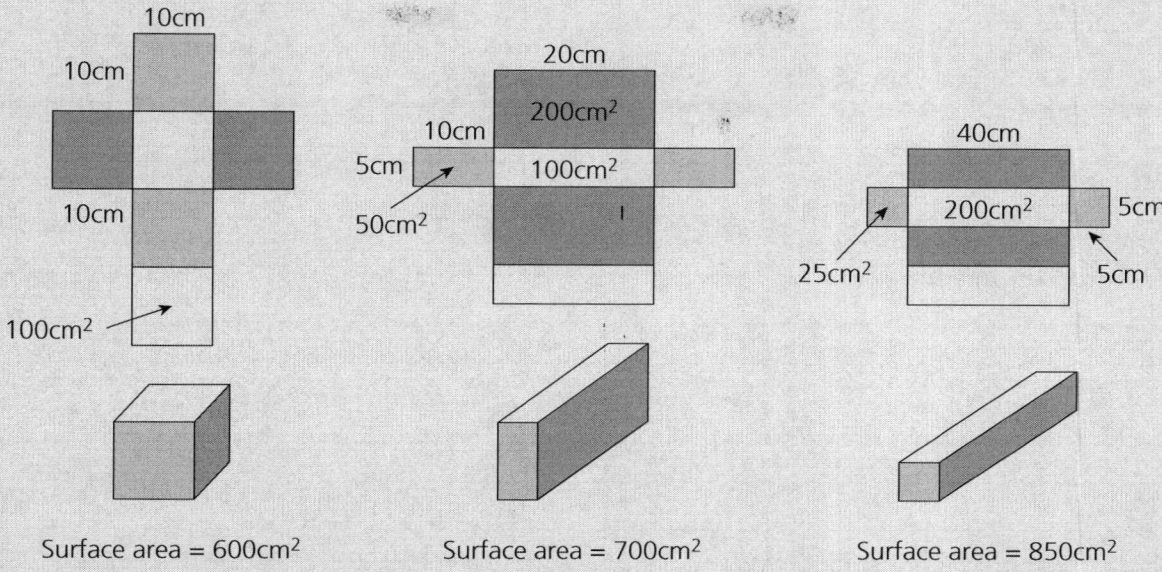

Surface area = 600cm²　　　　Surface area = 700cm²　　　　Surface area = 850cm²

Assessment

Pupils have been exploring how when rectangles and squares have the same perimeters, the longer and narrower the rectangle, the smaller its area and the square always has the greatest area. They should use this knowledge as a basis for mathematical reasoning in this problem and make an initial conjecture that the closer the cuboid gets to being a cube, the smaller its surface area and ultimately the cube will have the smallest surface area.

They should then investigate the examples given by firstly calculating the areas of each of the panels making up the different nets and then finding their respective sums. Ask them which of the two non-cube cuboids they think is closer in look to a cube. Check that pupils have noticed that as a cuboid gets longer and narrower, its surface area gets bigger.

Encourage pupils to draw a cuboid with the same volume as the three in the challenge that might have a surface area between that of the cube and the cuboid in the middle of the diagram in the question. Check how they approach this task. Are they looking at the other cuboid to see if, for example, a height between 5cm and 10cm could be possible and how it would affect the other two dimensions? For example, if they chose a height of 8cm and kept the base of 5cm, can they determine the length of this new cuboid and, importantly, does its surface area fit somewhere between the surface areas of the cube and the middle cuboid?

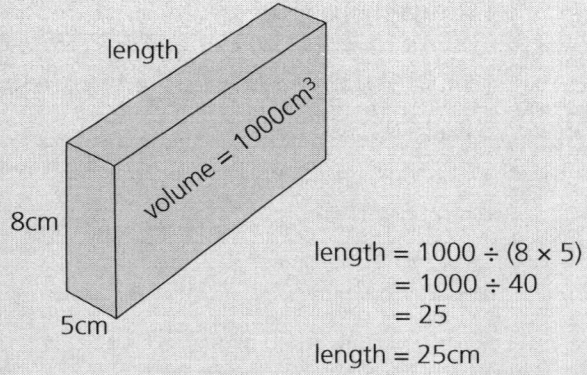

length = 1000 ÷ (8 × 5)
　　　 = 1000 ÷ 40
　　　 = 25
length = 25cm

Geometry – Properties of shape

Shaping up

Challenge 1: Which of the following are right-angled triangles and which are isosceles? Are any of them neither? Comment on each one, giving the reason for your answer. They are not accurately drawn.

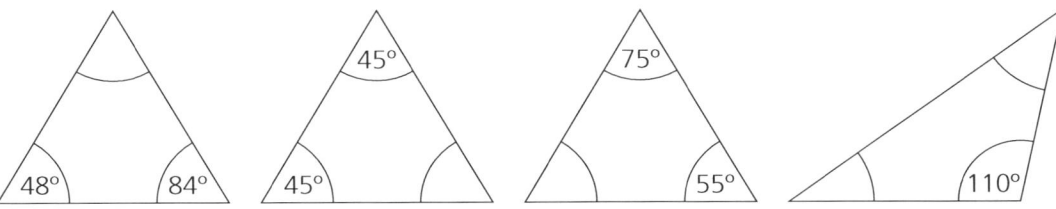

Challenge 2: Two equilateral triangles are arranged to make a star in the centre of an irregular hexagon.

a) How many different triangles are there in the diagram?

b) Label all the angles that you can without using a protractor.

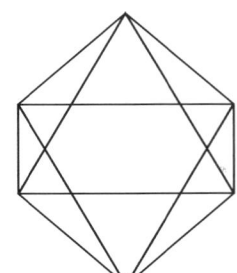

Challenge 3: Ineke says that if she drew a circle and measured an angle of 105° from the centre to the circumference then the arc it produced would be exactly $\frac{7}{24}$ of the circumference. Because she knows that 105° = 60° + 45° she says she used this to help her to come to this conclusion.

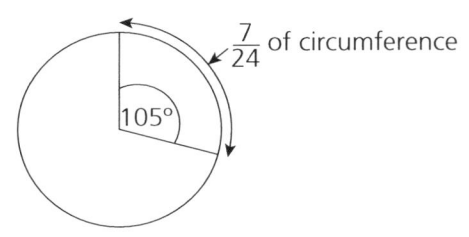

Is she correct? If so, how did she use the angles she mentioned to get to the result? Is there another way to check if she is correct?

Challenge 4: Here are two regular polygons, a pentagon and an octagon, with labelled angles. In both polygons, AB is a straight line.

Calculate the angles and explain how you know.

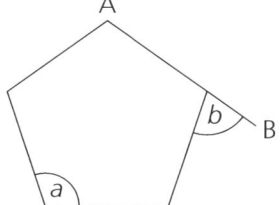

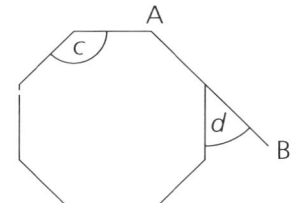

National Curriculum objectives, Year 6, Properties of shape

- **draw 2-D shapes using given dimensions and angles**
- **recognise, describe and build simple 3-D shapes, including making nets**
- **compare and classify geometric shapes based on their properties and sizes and find unknown angles in any triangles, quadrilaterals, and regular polygons**
- **illustrate and name parts of circles, including radius, diameter and circumference and know that the diameter is twice the radius**
- **recognise angles where they meet at a point, are on a straight line, or are vertically opposite, and find missing angles**

Challenge 1 Answer

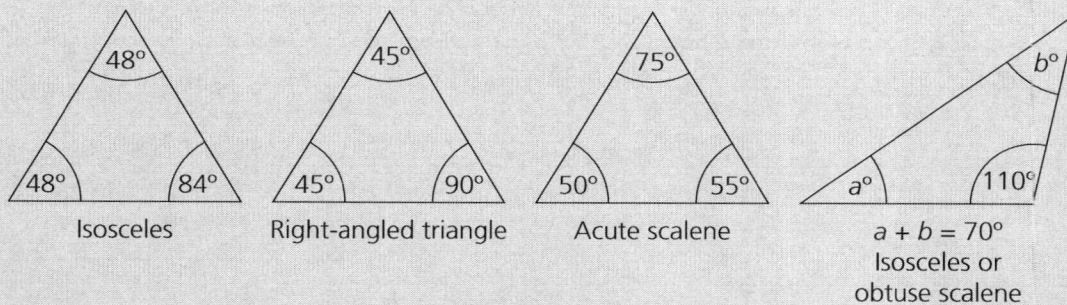

| Isosceles | Right-angled triangle | Acute scalene | $a + b = 70°$ Isosceles or obtuse scalene |

The first triangle is an isosceles because 180° – (48° + 84°) = 48° and isosceles triangles have two equal angles. The second is a right-angled isosceles because the given angles sum to 90° so the missing angle must be 90°. The third is an acute scalene triangle because all the angles are different and each one is less than 90°. The final triangle is either an obtuse scalene as one angle is greater than 90° and all three are different or an isosceles if $a = b$.

Assessment

Pupils should pay particular attention to the last sentence in the question as none of the triangles look like right-angled triangles. They should reason that they will need to use their knowledge that the sum of the interior angles of a triangle are 180°. Pupils with greater fluency of approach will be able to say that the two given angles must sum to 90° in order for it to be a right-angled triangle. After adding the angles given in each diagram, they should be able to make their statements as to which are right-angled triangles.

Check for pupils who use the reasoning that the units digits in the angles to be added must sum to 0 in order to total 90°. For example, they could reason that the first triangle cannot contain a 90° angle as 8 + 4 (units digits) sum to 12 (or a units digit of 2) and therefore this triangle cannot be a right-angled triangle.

Check for further examples of fluency from pupils who realise that the last triangle has an angle greater than a right angle and therefore the sum of the other two angles must be less than a right angle.

Challenge 2 Answer

a) The numbers below tell you how many of the shaded triangle there are in the whole shape. In the first one, there is just one equilateral triangle; in the last shape, there are four obtuse scalene triangles like the one shaded in the whole shape. If you add all the numbers above each example it sums to 32 triangles altogether.

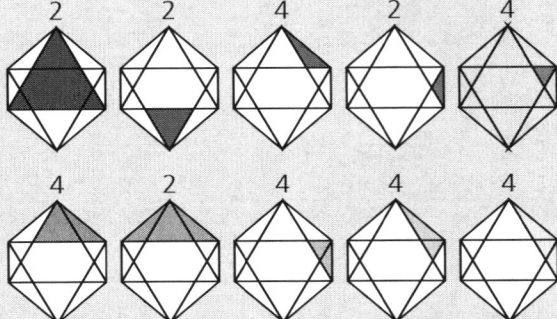

b)

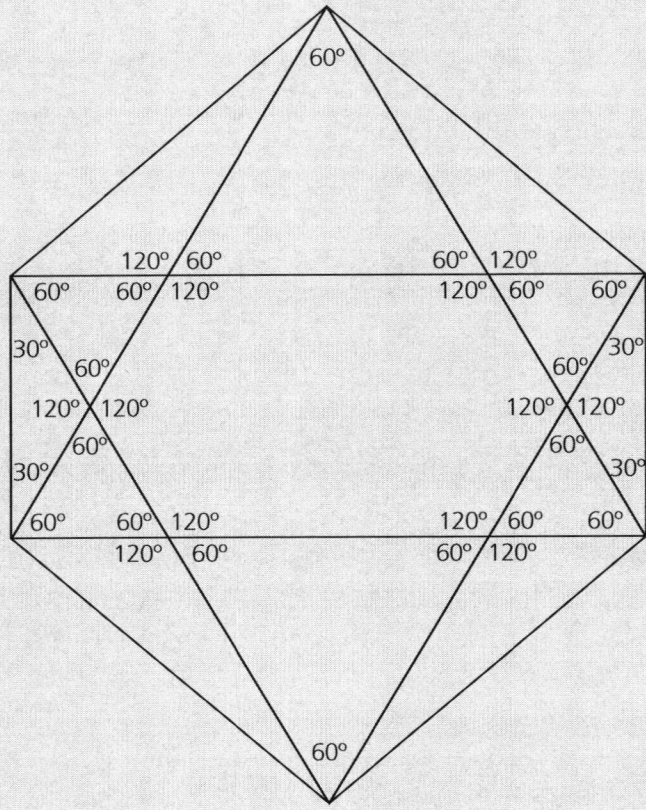

Assessment

In (a), pupils should use a systematic approach to search for every possible triangle. They should first find all the different single triangles, then move on to the compound triangles. They should realise that some will be repeated congruent triangles, due to the nature of the construction (two equilateral triangles in the shape of a six-pointed star bounded by a hexagon).

Pupils should see (b) as a set of problems solvable from known qualities within the shape. They will need to apply the knowledge that angles in equilateral triangles are all 60°, angles on a straight line total 180°, as do the sum of the interior angles of any triangle, and that where two straight lines cross, opposite angles are equal to each other. They should use this knowledge to make and test reasoned conjectures about unknown angles. A high level of reasoning is shown by arguing that the equilateral triangles forming the star can be moved vertically whilst maintaining the parallel nature of their bases and that an unmarked angle size is dependent upon the size of another unmarked corner in the same triangle. They should reason that moving equilateral triangles in this manner would not alter the marked angles.

Challenge 3 Answer

Ineke is correct, 105° is $\frac{7}{24}$ of the circumference.

Assessment

Pupils should confirm that the two stated angles (60° and 45°) are equal to 105°. Check that they are making direct links to fractions by looking at the angles 60° and 45° in terms of fractions of the angle in a complete circular turn (360°). If they do this, they should be able to confirm that it amounts to $\frac{1}{6}$ of a circle plus $\frac{1}{8}$ of a circle, which they should reason is the fraction of the whole circumference between the two angles.

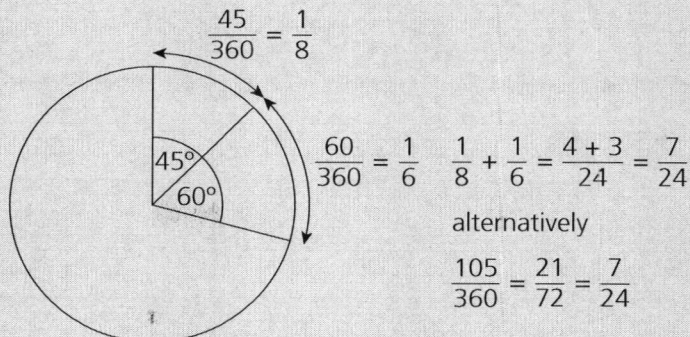

$$\frac{45}{360} = \frac{1}{8}$$

$$\frac{60}{360} = \frac{1}{6} \qquad \frac{1}{8} + \frac{1}{6} = \frac{4+3}{24} = \frac{7}{24}$$

alternatively

$$\frac{105}{360} = \frac{21}{72} = \frac{7}{24}$$

Check that they are able to add the fractions using a common denominator of 24 in order to confirm it is $\frac{7}{24}$ of the whole circumference.

Pupils should find different combinations of angles that sum to 105° to check Ineke is correct. Are their angles more useful than Ineke's? For example, $90° \left(\frac{1}{4}\right) + 15° \left(\frac{3}{72}\right) = 105°$, but does that make for a better fraction addition in their opinion? And does the resulting fraction also result in $\frac{7}{24}$?

Challenge 4 Answer

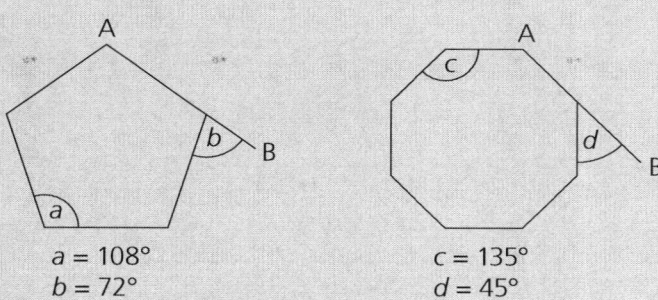

$a = 108°$
$b = 72°$

$c = 135°$
$d = 45°$

Assessment

Pupils should be able to reason that any polygon can be sectioned into a number of triangles using the polygons' existing vertices and apply their knowledge that angles in a triangle total 180°.

Check that they link this knowledge with the understanding that regular polygons have identical angles at each vertex, and realise that they could calculate these by dividing the sum of the angles in the triangles (540°) by 5 in the example of the pentagon. From here, pupils should reason that as a line measures 180° then the external angle is 180° minus the interior angle, so in the case of the regular pentagon it measures 72°.

They should use the same reasoning with the octagon.

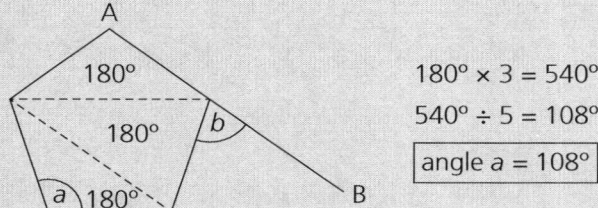

$180° \times 3 = 540°$

$540° \div 5 = 108°$

angle $a = 108°$

Geometry – Properties of shape

Coordinates, shapes and angles

Challenge 5: The two coordinates on the grid represent two vertices of an isosceles triangle.

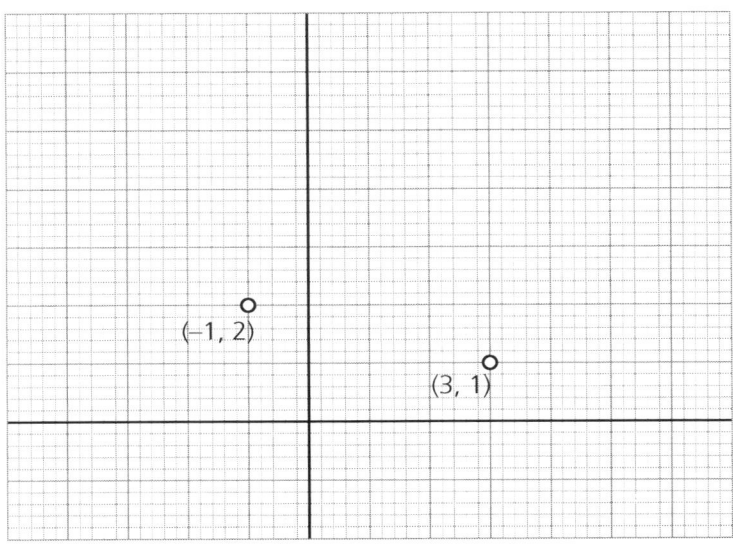

(−1, 2)

(3, 1)

a) How many coordinates can you find that could be the third in the isosceles triangle?

b) Are these the only possibilities? Explain your reasoning for this answer.

Challenge 6: If three angles of 120° are drawn from the centre of any circle to the circumference, then each part of the circumference will represent 33.3% or $\frac{1}{3}$ of its total length because $\frac{1}{3}$ of 360° is 120°.

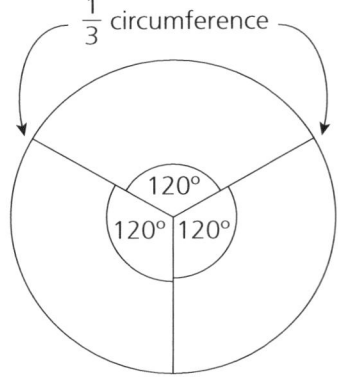

$\frac{1}{3}$ circumference

120°
120° 120°

Write the percentage of the circumference that the following angles from the centre to the circumference would produce. Give your answer to two decimal places if necessary.

a) 45°

b) 60°

c) 30° + 45°

d) 67.5° (Hint: which two angles could be added to get this angle?)

e) Is writing the result as a percentage of the circumference the best method to use? Explain why you think you are right.

Challenge 7: Three angles lie on a straight line in the diagram below. Calculate the value of the smallest angle on the line if the missing angles are all equal.

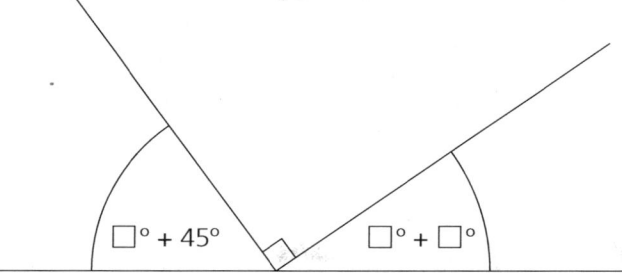

$\square° + 45°$ $\square° + \square°$

Challenge 8: The diagram below shows four triangles meeting at a point.

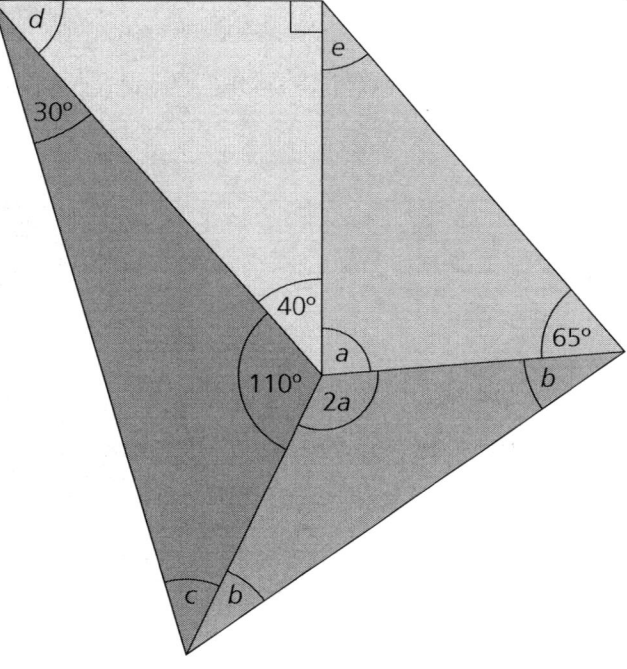

a) Calculate the unknown angles.

b) Work out what kind of triangle each one is and then label it. Explain why you think your labels are correct.

National Curriculum objectives, Year 6, Properties of shape

- *draw 2-D shapes using given dimensions and angles*
- *recognise, describe and build simple 3-D shapes, including making nets*

National Curriculum objectives, Year 6, Statistics

- *interpret and construct pie charts and line graphs and use these to solve problems*
- *calculate and interpret the mean as an average*

Challenge 1 Answer

a) 26 goals = 156°, 21 goals = 126°, 13 goals = 78°

b)

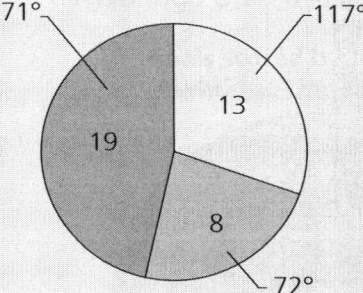

Assessment

Look for reasoning in (a) that the angles around the point at the centre of the pie chart sum to 360° and that if the numbers shown were added (26 + 21 + 13 = 60) and the result divided into 360, it would tell us the value of a 'goal' in terms of degrees on this pie chart (6). This is then multiplied by the number of goals to show the three sets of goal data in terms of angles in the pie chart.

Pupils should apply the same reasoning in (b).

Some pupils may be making links to ratio and proportion, which indicates a more fluent approach to the problem. For example, the diagram below shows how they might interpret the 26 goal data, showing that the 26 goals out of the total of 60 scored is proportionate to some number of degrees out of a total of 360. This will be achieved by pupils with higher level of understanding.

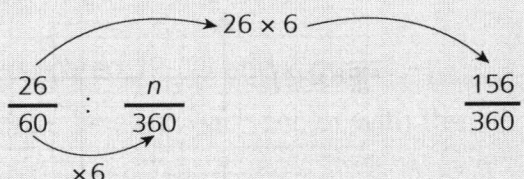

Challenge 2 Answer

a) The total of the two unknown heights (*a* and *b*) is 2.82m. This can be split into two different heights in many ways, for example 1.44m and 1.38m.

b) It is not true that the tallest member must be from the first team based only on that team's mean height. The sum of the heights is 4 × 1.4m = 5.6m. If the tallest member of the team was, for example, 1.46m then the three other members could each be 1.38m in height.

Assessment

In (a), look for pupils to reason that if the mean height of four athletes is 1.42m, then the total height is 4 × 1.42m = 5.68m. If the known heights are subtracted from this, pupils will be left with the combined height of the other two members (2.82m). Pupils should be able to divide this result by 2 (1.41m), but will be aware that this is not a possible answer as the two heights must be different. Check that pupils can subtract and add numbers to 1.41m so that the sum is always 2.82m; this will give a range of possible heights and show that there is more than one way of resolving the problem. Question the appropriateness of their answers – for example, 2.7m and 0.12m would satisfy the mean height figure, but are not realistic answers.

Pupils should explain their findings based on mathematical reasoning about the characteristics of right-angled triangles and reflective symmetry. Fluency can be assessed through the written approach to the problem with no evidence of a trial and improvement method.

Challenge 6 Answer

a)   12.5%

b)   16.67% (2 d.p.)

c)   20.83% (2 d.p.)

d)   18.75% (45° and 22.5°)

e)   It is easier and more accurate to use fractions as they give an exact number whereas decimals and percentages often have recurring decimal places.

Assessment

In (a), pupils should be able to link the size of the angle to a fraction of 360°, write this in its simplest form and then convert the result to a percentage via decimals. For example:

$$\frac{45°}{360°} = \frac{1}{8} = 0.125 = 12.5\%$$

In (b), they should calculate that the fraction representing the angle is $\frac{1}{6}$ and then use formal division to calculate that this gives a recurring decimal (0.1666666…), which can be written as 16.67% to two decimal places. Ask pupils who write the result as 16.66% to explain how they got to that result.

In (c), pupils should be working with the fractions $\frac{1}{12}$ and $\frac{1}{8}$, which combine to a total of $\frac{5}{24}$ of the circumference. Through further long division and conversion they should get the result 20.83% to two decimal places.

$$\frac{1}{12} + \frac{1}{8} = \frac{2}{24} + \frac{3}{24} = \frac{5}{24}$$

Check in (d) that pupils have separated the angle into 45° and found half of that (22.5°) for a fluent and well-reasoned approach. This leaves two relatively easy fractions to add $\left(\frac{1}{8} + \frac{1}{16} = \frac{3}{16}\right)$, which through long division takes them to the percentage 18.75%. If they are having trouble searching for the two angles, direct them to look for 'friendly' angles that could be part of the sum (like 45°, without actually mentioning it).

Part (e) is assessing mathematical reasoning and fluency of approach to problem solving. Pupils should know that fractions, percentages and decimals can be used to represent the same number. Check that pupils can argue that as fractions are (more often than not) required in order to get to a decimal equivalent, it would seem appropriate to record results as fractions.

Challenge 7 Answer

The empty boxes represent 15° so the smallest angle is 30° and is the one to the right of the right angle.

Assessment

Look for pupils' mathematical reasoning in this task. Check that they are breaking the problem down systematically. Do they start with the straight line on which all the angles lie and the knowledge that the angles must total 180°? Are they systematically using the knowledge that the two angles with unknown parts must total 90°? From this reasoning, are they able to calculate that the three unknown angles must total 90 − 45 = 45 and as such the unknown angles are each 15°?

The bar method would explain the reasoning behind how the missing angles are calculated.

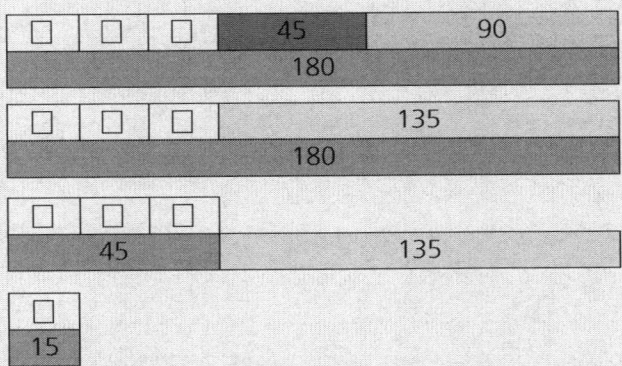

Pupils showing a greater level of fluency and mastery will identify the problem in algebraic terms and solve the equation $3n + 135 = 180$, replacing the unknown empty box with a letter and applying equal operations to both sides until it is revealed that $n = 15$.

Ask pupils if they could calculate the unknowns if the angle on the left-hand side was labelled 30° instead of 45°. Challenge them further by asking them to calculate the unknown angles if the right angle in the centre was replaced with the sum of two boxes (box = 27°).

Challenge 8 Answer

a) $a = 70°$, $2a = 140°$, $b = 20°$, $c = 40°$, $d = 50°$, $e = 45°$

b)

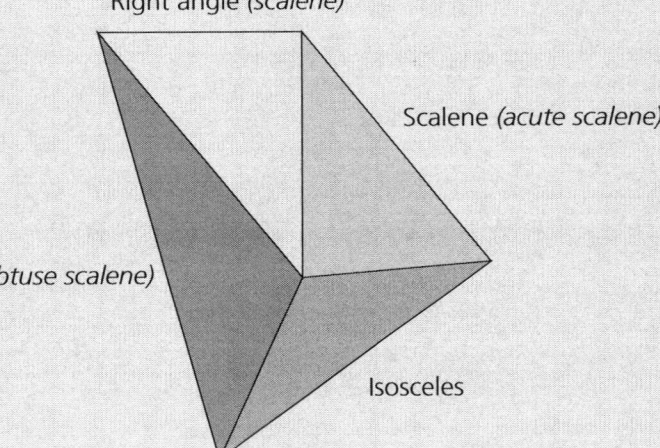

Right angle *(scalene)*

Scalene *(acute scalene)*

Scalene *(obtuse scalene)*

Isosceles

Assessment

In problem (a), pupils might start by reasoning that as the triangles meet at a point, the sum of the angles around it will be 360°. After adding the given angles (110° and 40°), they will subtract this from 360° to calculate the remaining angle around the point (210°). Dividing this by 3 will give enough information to calculate the values of a and $2a$.

Alternatively, pupils may start by calculating angles c and d from what is known about the sum of the angles in a triangle.

The remaining angles will then be calculated by subtracting each of the known angles from 180°.

Pupils demonstrating fluency will check their results using the knowledge that the four triangles form a quadrilateral with four corners that sum to 360°.

In problem (b), pupils will use understanding of the characteristics of triangles to label the triangles and explain their reasoning. Pupils demonstrating a high level of mathematical reasoning will be able to label the isosceles triangle ($2a$, b and b) before the numerical values are found. An acceptable level of fluency will be demonstrated if each triangle is labelled without the extra information given in brackets in the answer; labelling the right-angled triangle as a right-angled scalene triangle shows a higher degree of mastery of the qualities of different triangles.

Geometry – Position and direction

Moving around

Challenge 1: The triangle in the diagram below has vertices labelled A, B and C. The triangle is to be translated so that the vertex A moves to the point marked 'x'.

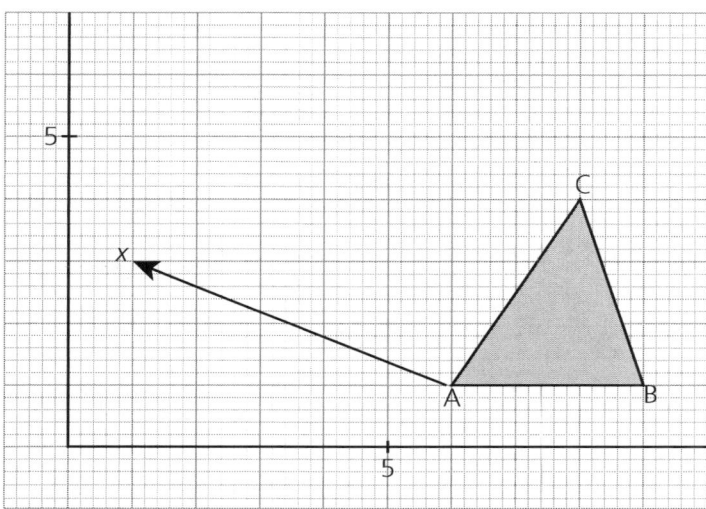

a) Write down the current vertices A, B and C as coordinates.

b) Write the new coordinates after the translation has taken place.

c) What do you notice about the x- and y-coordinates of the corresponding vertices? Is there a pattern?

d) If vertex A in the original triangle is translated to the coordinate (−2, 2), what are the new coordinates of the other two vertices?

Challenge 2: The irregular pentagon shown to the right has its coordinates labelled so you can make an exact copy. Paul and Jackie reflect the shape in the y-axis. They then reflect both shapes in the x-axis. Paul says the outline of the shape now on the axes is a rectangle. Jackie disagrees. What shape do you think is now on the axes?

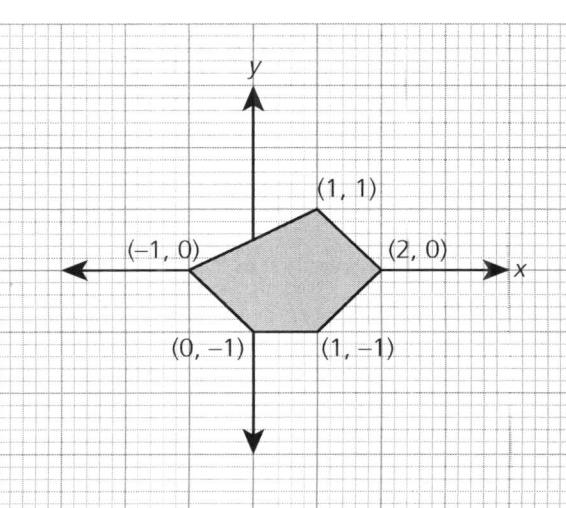

Challenge 3: Copy the diagram below.

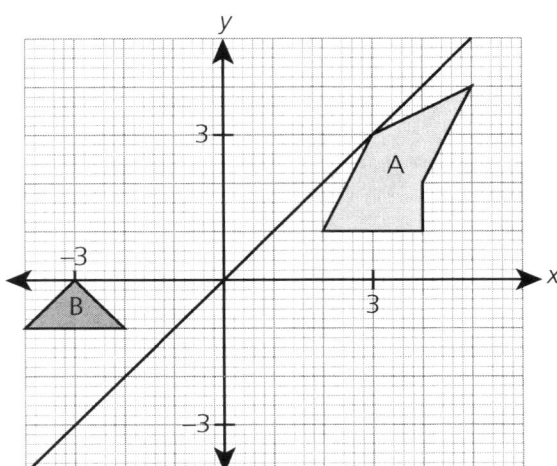

Label the coordinates of each vertex in shape A, then reflect it in the diagonal line.

Label the vertices of the reflected shape. What do you notice?

Use any number patterns you might notice to reflect shape B in the same diagonal line.

Look at each of the coordinates (x, y) of the points on the line of reflection. What do you notice? Make a rule based on what you see.

Look at the following coordinate points and decide what the new coordinate points would be if they were reflected in the diagonal line.

a) (−1, 1) **b)** (−1, 2) **c)** (0, 2) **d)** (3.5, −0.5)

Challenge 4: Jon thinks that if the two coordinates (3, 4) and (−2, 5) on the diagram below are given as two vertices of an irregular quadrilateral then there are at least two more vertices that we can use that show a quadrilateral with a total of three acute angles.

Do you agree or do you think it is not possible? Explain how you know. You can use a protractor to measure your angles.

Jon also says that the only quadrilateral with two obtuse and two acute angles is a parallelogram. Show an example to prove that he is wrong, then explain why his statement is incorrect.

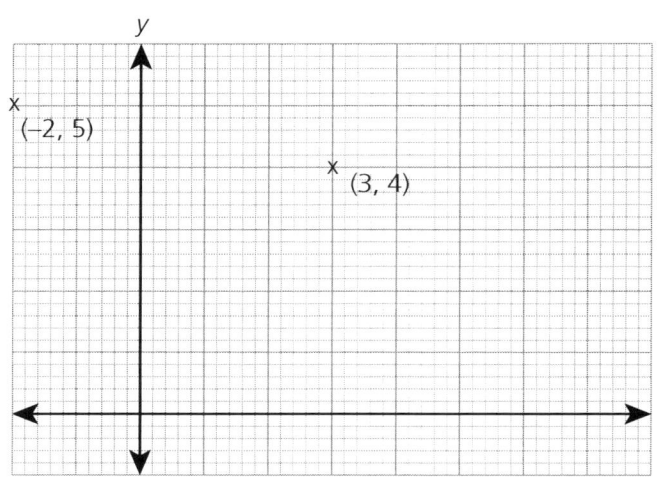

National Curriculum objectives, Year 6, Position and direction

- *describe positions on the full coordinate grid (all four quadrants)*
- *draw and translate simple shapes on the coordinate plane, and reflect them in the axes*

Challenge 1 Answer

a)   A (6, 1), B (9, 1) and C (8, 4)

b)   A (6, 1) to **(1, 3)**, B (9, 1) to **(4, 3)** and C (8, 4) to **(3, 6)**

c)   The *x*-coordinate on all of them is 5 less than the original and the *y*-coordinate is 2 greater than the original.

d)   B (9, 1) to **(1, 2)** and C (8, 4) to **(0, 5)**

Assessment

Look for reasoning from pupils that translation of a shape means that every point on the shape moves to a new position using a constant rule. Look for pupils seeing the translation not as an oblique movement, but rather movement in the *x*-direction (horizontal) followed by a move in the *y*-direction (vertical). Check that when the movement or rule has been identified, it is applied to each vertex in the shape.

Challenge 2 Answer

In the following diagrams, **a** shows the initial reflection in the *y*-axis and **b** shows the resulting outline. This outline shape is then reflected in the *x*-axis, as shown in **c**. Finally, after all the transformations, we can see that the new outline shape produced, **d**, is a hexagon.

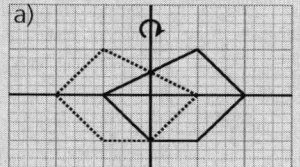 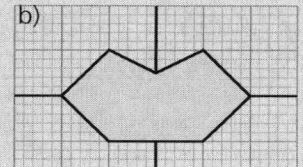 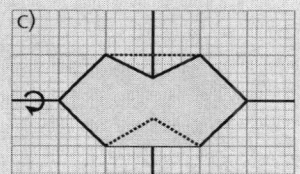 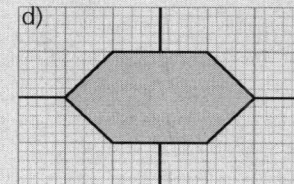

Assessment

Look for reasoning from pupils that when reflecting a shape in a given axis, all points on one side follow a rule that takes them to the other side. This is quite challenging when the line of reflection cuts through the shape to be reflected, but by maintaining the rule pupils should achieve success.

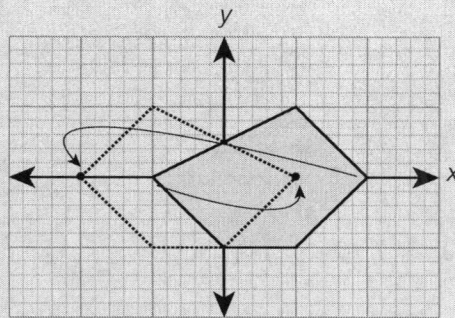

Make sure that pupils recognise and use the fact that vertices reflected in the *y*-axis will contain the same digits in the reflected coordinate, except that the *x* value will be a negative value of its original position. In the diagram to the right, for example, (2, 0) reflected in the *y*-axis becomes (–2, 0). Likewise, a reflection in the *x*-axis has the effect of changing the *y* value in the coordinate to a negative of its original value.

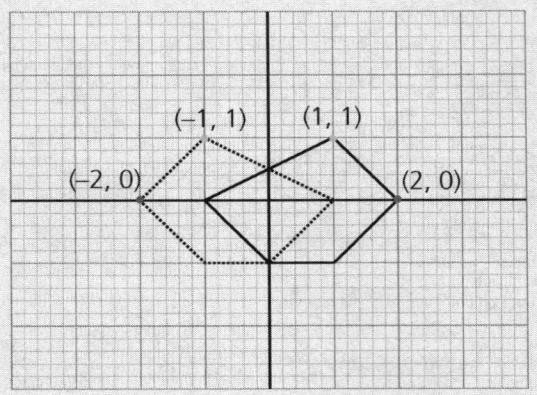

Check that pupils reason that the same process applies to the subsequent reflections, resulting in a final shape that is a hexagon and not a rectangle as stated.

Ask pupils to explain how they conceptually understood how the reflection worked in this challenge. For example, do some pupils understand the problem in three-dimensions and realise that if the shape was freely able to rotate around a rod (a good model for the *y*-axis) then a rotation of 180° would effectively represent the reflection demanded in the challenge, which is in two-dimensions?

Challenge 3 Answer

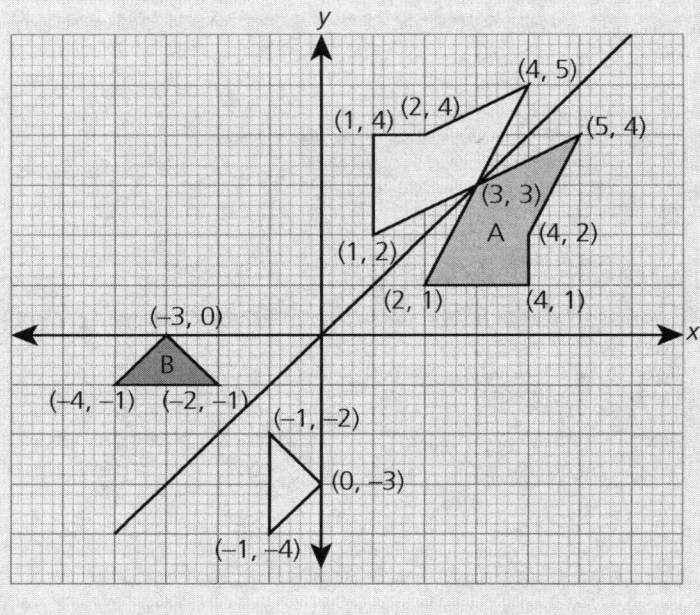

a) (1, –1) **b)** (2, –1) **c)** (2, 0) **d)** (–0.5, 3.5)

Assessment

Check that pupils understand that when any point is reflected in a given line, the reflection will be perpendicular to the line of reflection. They should use this knowledge to count how many diagonals there are between each vertex and the given line and then repeat this on the other side to arrive at its reflected position.

Check that they have noticed that the reflected coordinates have changed from *x*-coordinate to *y*-coordinate and vice versa. Ask pupils if we can name the line of reflection $x = y$ or $y = x$ and if this would fit what we noticed about how the coordinates are affected when they get reflected in this line. If they are not sure, ask them to select three random points on the line and write the coordinate values to see if this convinces them.

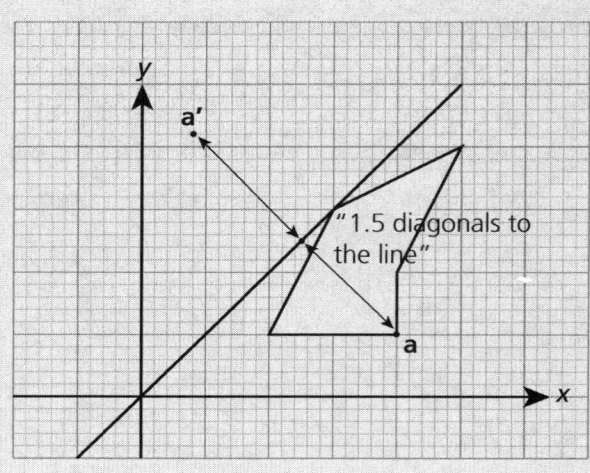

Challenge 4 Answer

These two examples show one quadrilateral with three acute angles and one obtuse angle, and one quadrilateral with three acute angles and one reflex angle. These examples are two of many depending on how many quadrants are used and whether the coordinates are restricted to whole number values.

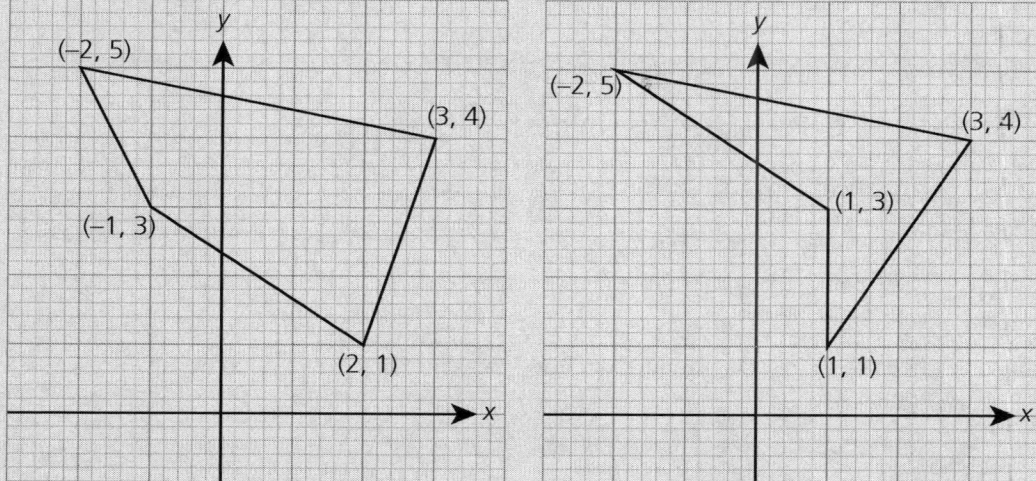

This example shows a quadrilateral with two obtuse and two acute angles that is not a parallelogram. Notice that the question does not require the labelling of the other two coordinates, which allows greater freedom to concentrate on measurement of angles.

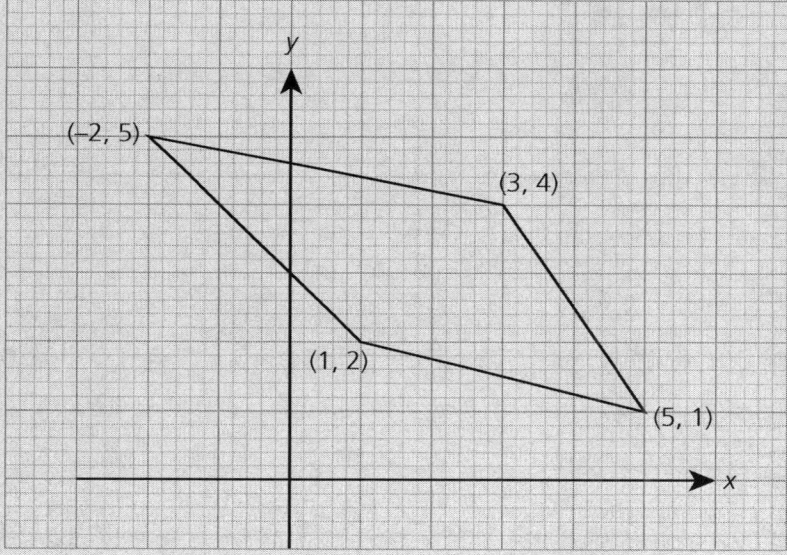

Assessment

Pupils should be able to reason that the sum of the angles inside any quadrilateral is 360° because a quadrilateral can be sectioned into two triangles each containing exactly 180°. They should use this understanding to calculate possible angles that will or will not fit the criteria of the different parts of the problem. For example, they may measure an obtuse angle from one of the given coordinates and subtract this from 360°. This figure can then either be divided by 3, giving three identical acute angles, or divided into three angles, all less than 90°, which sum to the remaining angle after the subtraction of the obtuse angle. A systematic approach like this will eradicate random attempts to arrive at solutions.

In showing an example of why Jon's statement is incorrect, expect to see an irregular quadrilateral, possibly with angles labelled 'acute' and 'obtuse'. Reasoning for why the statement is incorrect will say that as all the angles total 360° this is the only important rule. They will argue that parallelograms have opposite angles equal to each other, but a quadrilateral can still have two unequal obtuse angles and two unequal acute angles with the only rule being they must total 360°.

Statistics

Averaging things out

Challenge 1: The pie chart below shows the number of goals scored by the top three goal scorers of Awbridge United last season.

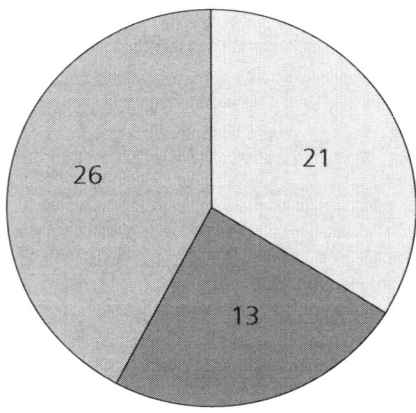

Goals scored by top strikers at Awbridge United last season

a) What are the angles on the pie chart for each of the goal scorers?

b) The season before, the top three goal scorers scored 19, 13 and 8 goals respectively. Draw a pie chart to show this data, labelling each sector with the number of goals and the angle.

Challenge 2: The mean height of four members of a junior tennis team is 1.42m. The tallest member of the group is 1.45m and the smallest is 1.41m. The heights of the other two members are not the same.

a) What could their heights be? Is there more than one answer to this?

b) Adrian says that in another team of four, the mean height is 1.4m and because of this, the tallest member of that team cannot be taller than the tallest member of the first team. Do you agree? How can you convince someone that you are correct?

Challenge 3: The mean midday temperature from Monday to Friday was recorded as 8.5°C. A graph is drawn of this data, but the temperature for Tuesday is missing. Is it possible to calculate this missing piece of data?

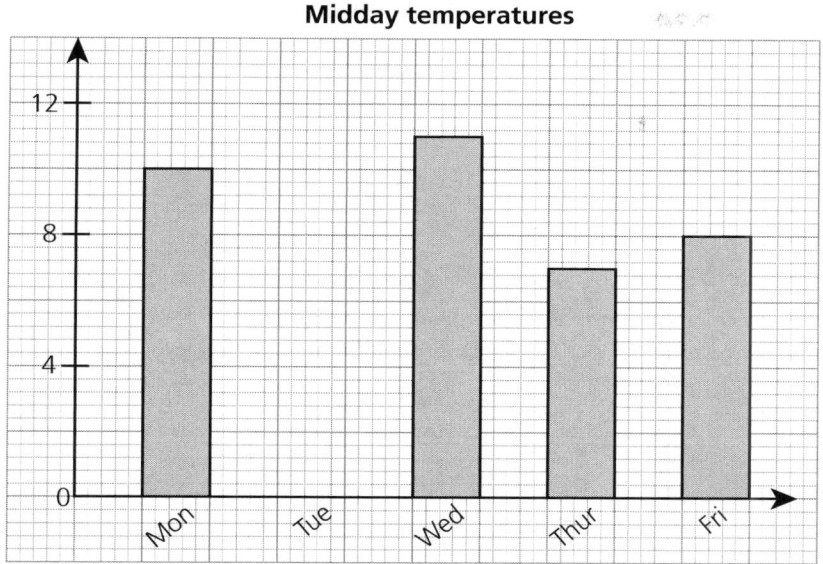

Challenge 4: The line graph shows the tariffs of two different car parks in a city centre. Car park A costs £2 to enter followed by a 50p per hour charge. Car park B charges a flat rate of £5 for a whole day.

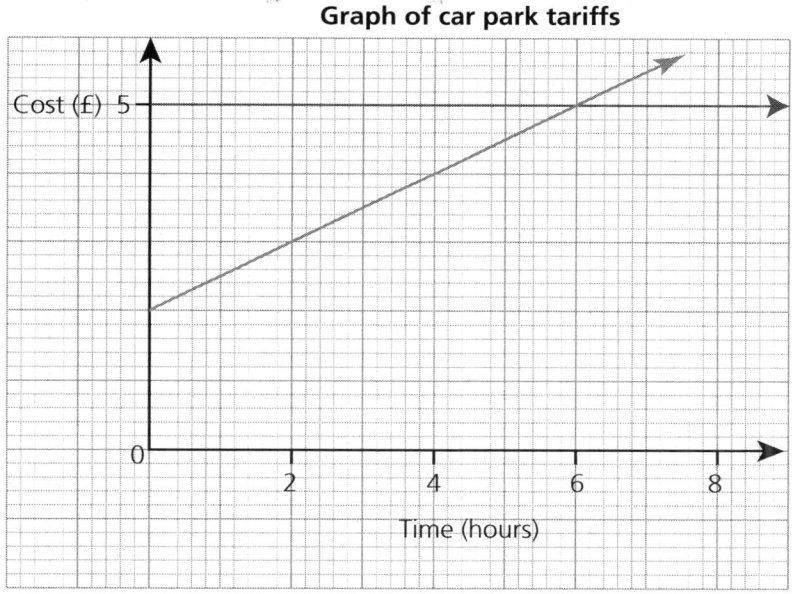

a) Label the lines A and B.

b) Which car park would you choose if you wanted to stay for 7.5 hours?

c) Which would you choose if you wanted to stay 4.5 hours?

d) When is car park A the best value for money?

e) How would the graph help you if you knew you wanted to stay for 7 hours?

National Curriculum objectives, Year 6, Statistics

- *interpret and construct pie charts and line graphs and use these to solve problems*
- *calculate and interpret the mean as an average*

Challenge 1 Answer

a) 26 goals = 156°, 21 goals = 126°, 13 goals = 78°

b)

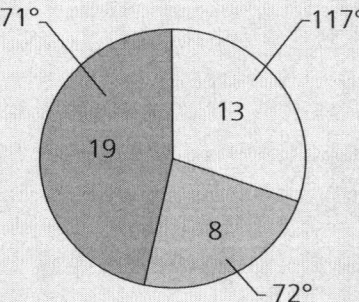

Assessment

Look for reasoning in (a) that the angles around the point at the centre of the pie chart sum to 360° and that if the numbers shown were added (26 + 21 + 13 = 60) and the result divided into 360, it would tell us the value of a 'goal' in terms of degrees on this pie chart (6). This is then multiplied by the number of goals to show the three sets of goal data in terms of angles in the pie chart.

Pupils should apply the same reasoning in (b).

Some pupils may be making links to ratio and proportion, which indicates a more fluent approach to the problem. For example, the diagram below shows how they might interpret the 26 goal data, showing that the 26 goals out of the total of 60 scored is proportionate to some number of degrees out of a total of 360. This will be achieved by pupils with higher level of understanding.

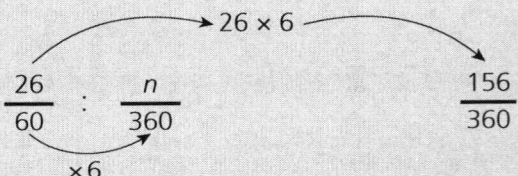

Challenge 2 Answer

a) The total of the two unknown heights (*a* and *b*) is 2.82m. This can be split into two different heights in many ways, for example 1.44m and 1.38m.

b) It is not true that the tallest member must be from the first team based only on that team's mean height. The sum of the heights is 4 × 1.4m = 5.6m. If the tallest member of the team was, for example, 1.46m then the three other members could each be 1.38m in height.

Assessment

In (a), look for pupils to reason that if the mean height of four athletes is 1.42m, then the total height is 4 × 1.42m = 5.68m. If the known heights are subtracted from this, pupils will be left with the combined height of the other two members (2.82m). Pupils should be able to divide this result by 2 (1.41m), but will be aware that this is not a possible answer as the two heights must be different. Check that pupils can subtract and add numbers to 1.41m so that the sum is always 2.82m; this will give a range of possible heights and show that there is more than one way of resolving the problem. Question the appropriateness of their answers – for example, 2.7m and 0.12m would satisfy the mean height figure, but are not realistic answers.

Knowing that the two athletes are different heights, some pupils may form the equation $a + b = 2.82$, and give a value to a in order to calculate b.

In (b), pupils should use the same method as (a) and simply show one example of why the statement is false.

Challenge 3 Answer

Yes. By multiplying the mean (8.5°C) by 5 (42.5°C) then subtracting the sum of the known temperatures (36°C), Tuesday's temperature can be calculated to be 6.5°C.

Assessment

Look for links to algebra when pupils calculate the answer to this problem.

Check that they add all the recorded temperatures from their reading of each bar on the graph ($10 + 11 + 7 + 8 = 36$) and encourage them to try to put the information they have into a simple equation form: Tuesday + 36 = 8.5 × 5. Check that they can simplify this to $t + 36 = 42.5$ and then calculate the result for Tuesday (t) by subtracting 36 from both sides.

The bar method could be used to illustrate the reasoning behind the rules of calculation in this problem.

Mon	Tue	Wed	Thur	Fri
10	n	11	7	8
		$5 \times 8.5 = 42.5$		

Mon	+	Tue	+	Wed	+	Thur	+	Fri
n								
6.5				36				

Challenge 4 Answer

a)

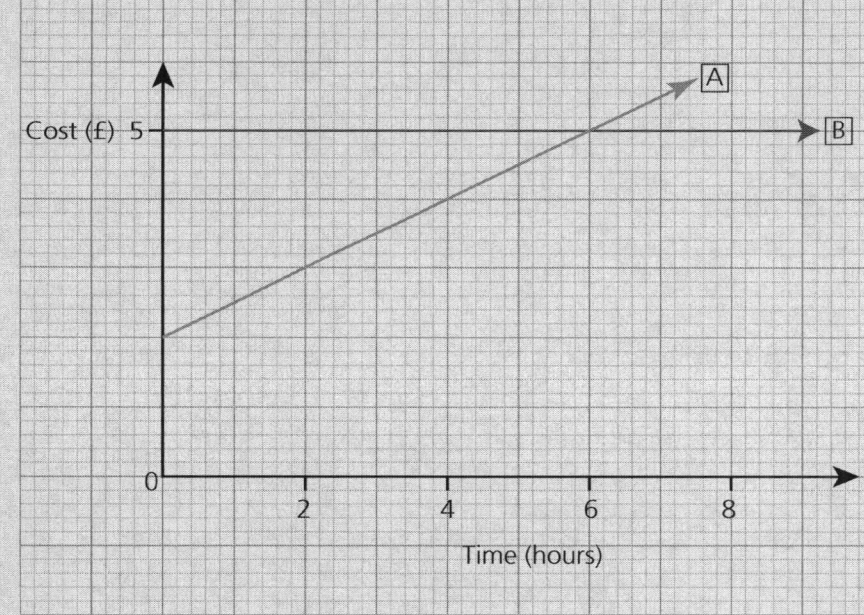

b)   Car park B

c)   Car park A

d)   Car park A is the best one to choose if you do not want to stay for more than six hours.

e)   You go to 7 on the time axis, then move vertically from there until you hit line A or B. The first line you touch is the car park that gives the best value for money.

Assessment

Check that in (a), pupils identify the horizontal line as showing the all-day cost of £5 because the cost is £5 at any point on the line, regardless of time spent there. They should reason from this that the other line must be car park A.

In (b), check that pupils are finding 7.5 hours on the x-axis and then moving parallel to the y-axis until they 'hit' a line. Can they convince you that the first line they hit is the best option?

Quiz pupils about their reasons for choosing car park A or B in (c). Did they use the reasoning, for example, that car park A is the first line you 'hit' when moving up from 4.5 hours on the x-axis?

In (d), pupils should argue that car park A is the best value for a stay of up to six hours because this is the time when both lines cross – so any time less than six hours is cheaper in car park A than the £5 being charged by car park B.

The reasoning behind the answer to (e) should link closely to that used in (b) and (c), which allows pupils to prove that the line to choose is always the first one they hit when moving up from any selected time. They should intuitively think that car park B is the answer because it is £5 all day and this in turn should guide them to the proof.